Will the Internet Fragment?

Digital Futures Series

Milton Mueller, *Will the Internet Fragment?*
Neil Selwyn, *Is Technology Good for Education?*

Will the Internet Fragment?

Sovereignty, Globalization, and Cyberspace

MILTON MUELLER

polity

First published in 2017 by Polity Press

Polity Press
65 Bridge Street
Cambridge CB2 1UR, UK

Polity Press
350 Main Street
Malden, MA 02148, USA

ISBN-13: 978-1-5095-0121-2 (hardback)
ISBN-13: 978-1-5095-0122-9 (paperback)

A catalogue record for this book is available from the British Library.

Typeset in 11 on 15 Adobe Garamond by
Servis Filmsetting Ltd, Stockport, Cheshire
Printed and bound in the UK by Clays Ltd, St Ives Plc

For further information on Polity, visit our website: politybooks.com

CONTENTS

ONE

Coming Undone?

An alarming message about the Internet is being voiced around the world. The Internet is in danger of splitting up, fragmenting. "After 20 years of connecting the world ever more tightly," the *Financial Times* wrote in late 2014, "the Internet is about to become Balkanised" (FT Reporters, 2014). A year later, two respected legal scholars lamented that "The era of a global Internet may be passing. Governments across the world are putting up barriers to the free flow of information across borders ... breaking apart the World Wide Web" (Chander and Le, 2015). The most apocalyptic vision came from cybersecurity expert Eugene Kaspersky, who claimed that "Internet fragmentation will bring about a paradoxical de-globalization of the world, as communications within national borders among governmental bodies and large national companies become increasingly localized" (Kaspersky, 2013, December 17).

How serious are these claims? There is certainly a political backlash against trade, immigration, and the European Union that seems to match these concerns about the Internet. How much of a threat, if any, do current trends in information and Internet policy pose to globalization? The more the idea of fragmentation or Balkanization plays a role in global Internet governance debates, the more important it becomes to interrogate those concepts. What do we really mean by Internet fragmentation? What are its manifestations? Is there really a risk that the global Internet could be divided up into distinct fiefdoms?

Engaging with these questions opens up a rich set of issues in communications policy and global governance. What seemed at first to be a simple dichotomy – globalized vs. territorialized information, an "open" vs. a "closed" Internet – turned out to be much more complex. Many of the things being called fragmentation are indeed destructive attempts by political authorities or private monopolies to limit and control the potential of information technology. But at the same time, many of the methods and techniques used for these bad purposes are also used by legitimate local actors to enhance or protect their own networks and their users' security and freedom of action. The basic, yet hard-to-grasp fact is that digital technology is so flexible and powerful that it enables both types of limitations in a variety of contexts.

"Fragmentation" is really the wrong word with which to approach this problem. In this book I will argue that the network effects and economic benefits of global compatibility are so powerful that they have consistently defeated, and will continue to defeat, any systemic deterioration of the global technical compatibility that the public Internet created. The rhetoric of "fragmentation" is in some ways a product of confusion, and in other ways an attempt to camouflage another, more inflammatory issue: the attempt by governments to align the Internet with their jurisdictional boundaries. The fragmentation debate is really a power struggle over the future of national sovereignty in the digital world. It's not just about the Internet. It's about geopolitics, national power, and the future of global governance.

The "unified and unfragmented space"

Turn the clock back to Sao Paulo, Brazil, in April 2014. Nearly 2,000 people from business, government, civil society, and the technical community converged on this city to discuss Internet governance. The meeting, dubbed the NETMundial by its proud Brazilian hosts, was a bold attempt to bring together a community both shocked and mobilized by Edward Snowden's revelations of NSA spying. One of the instigators of the meeting, Fadi Chehadé, at that time the President and CEO of ICANN, announced, "If we cannot find a way to govern the Internet on an equal footing, in an open transparent way this year, we might descend into a fragmented version of the Internet" (Chehadé, 2014).

Reacting to the news that the Internet had become a tool of globalized, mass surveillance, the NETMundial congregated to forge agreement on some basic principles for global Internet governance. Though many of the principles debated at the meeting proved contentious, it had no trouble coming to consensus on this one:

UNIFIED AND UNFRAGMENTED SPACE
The Internet should continue to be a globally coherent, interconnected, stable, unfragmented, scalable and accessible network-of-networks, based on a common set of unique identifiers ... that allows data packets/information to flow freely end-to-end ... (NETMundial 2014)

However awkwardly phrased, the principle that the Internet should be unified and unfragmented was considered fundamental; it sat in the event's outcome

"The fragmentation debate is really a power struggle over the future of national sovereignty in the digital world."

document alongside principles such as HUMAN RIGHTS and SECURITY, STABILITY AND RESILIENCE.

NETMundial was only one of the many manifestations of a world-embracing universalism or globalizing tendency that has always been present in the technical vision of the Internet. One of the inventors of the Internet protocols, Vinton G. Cerf, wrote:

> From a technical standpoint, the original shared vision guiding the Internet's development was that every device on the Internet should be able to exchange data packets with any other device that was willing to receive them. Universal connectivity among the willing was the default assumption . . . (Drake, Cerf, and Kleinwachter, 2015)

One of the most strident advocates of this vision is the designer of the World Wide Web protocol, Tim Berners-Lee. Berners-Lee believes that the Web is a universe that is (or should be – for the line between the normative and the positive is always fuzzy when computer scientists talk about policy) subject to uniform laws, which he compares matter-of-factly to the laws of physics:

Ants, Neurons, objects, particles, people. In each case, the whole operates only because the parts interoperate. The behaviour of the whole is in some way dictated by the rules of behaviour of the parts. This may be a view influenced too much by physics, but I find it useful. It makes you think about how you predict the rules of the whole from the rules of the parts, and then as a global engineer (constitution writer, etc) how you can phrase the local laws to engender the global behaviour he desires. For people, we call these rules variously the constitution, laws, or codes of ethics, for example. These rules are things which are accepted across the board. For particles, we call them the laws of physics. For web objects they are the protocol standards. (Berners-Lee, 1995)

Berners-Lee, and many others like him, hold up as a guiding norm the idea that "an application should function at one point in the network as it does at any other; a website should look the same to a person in China as it does to a person in Chile. In other words, the experience of every Internet user should be the same regardless of geographic location, computer type, or any other distinguishing characteristic of the user" (Hill, 2012).

This "laws of physics" approach is echoed by the Internet Society's description of the essential features of the Internet – what they call, again echoing the language of mathematical axioms or natural laws, one of the "Internet invariants."

> Global reach, integrity: Any endpoint of the Internet can address any other endpoint, and the information received at one endpoint is as intended by the sender, wherever the receiver connects to the Internet. Implicit in this is the requirement of global, managed addressing and naming services. (Daigle, 2015)

This commitment to perfect interoperability, to a seamlessly interconnected, borderless, and transparent cyberspace, is not a recent turn. It is an almost religious principle of the Internet technical community, built into its DNA. The US Department of Defense (DoD) funded the development of the Internet protocols not, as is commonly assumed, so that the network would survive a nuclear war, but because it wanted its field personnel to be able to communicate seamlessly regardless of what system or physical medium they were using. DoD wanted a single protocol to unify – to internetwork – any and all of their data communications.

They got one, and more. The community of computer scientists and network engineers they funded bought into the principle of interoperability with a fervor that exceeded the military's original intent. And their commitment to that principle proved to be right. The economic and social benefits of interoperability among civilians and businesses in a digitizing world vastly exceeded its minor contribution to US military communications. In the 1980s, when personal computers and other digital devices began to proliferate, the open, nonproprietary Internet protocols met a powerful need. It took only about a dozen years for the Internet protocols, officially standardized late in 1981 and implemented from 1982 to 1984, to take over the world of digital communications completely. From about 1993 on, adoption of the Internet protocols reached the critical mass needed to create the bandwagon effect of self-sustaining growth. The Internet succeeded precisely because it overcame the compatibility barriers – the technical fragmentation – of the world of national telephone monopolies and multiple proprietary data networking protocols into which it was born.

The mismatch

Though rooted in the ideals of the technical community, the "unfragmented space" was a vision with profound political and economic implications. It is a vision that militates against jurisdictional boundaries on the flow of information. It is a vision that, if carried out consistently, drastically diminishes the power of local politicians and governments to shape and control information. With respect to the information economy, it is globalization on steroids. A system that is engineered to make communications and information accessible and interoperable across the board enables commercial exchanges of digital goods and information services among any two connected parties. In other words, it implies pure free trade in information services, a globalized market unprotected by customs checkpoints or tariffs. In a unified and unfragmented space, any entrepreneur with a new idea can make the world their marketplace. Turning the tables on the state, it moves from a regime requiring prior permission from national regulators to a regime of permissionless innovation (Thierer, 2014). As one Internet technologist put it, "The Internet was not designed to recognize national boundaries. It's not being rude – they just weren't relevant" (Daigle, 2013).

Of course, the technology *also* enables its users to *opt out* of any particular exchange of information. It provides all kinds of means by which those who are *not* willing to accept packets from others can block them. And that is where the quasi-religious fervor for global compatibility meets its moderating principle.

It has become a cliché to note that the "unified and unfragmented space" created by the victory of the Internet protocols was filled not only with innovative economic and social activity, but also with the crimes and conflicts that accompany human interactions in every other space. Along with the innovations, efficiencies, and creative new forms of entertainment and interaction came thieves, bullies, fraudsters, child abusers, spies, vandals. Most of the time, but not always, our services and devices can be configured to restrict these kinds of abuses, but usually only after the fact. But this litany of Internet-related problems rarely pauses to ask why these problems are so unique and disruptive.

Internet governance is hard not simply because networked digital devices have created all kinds of new problems, but also because of the *mismatch* between its global scope and the *political and legal institutions* for responding to societal problems. The state, law, policies, regulations, and courts are human society's primary mechanism for handling crime and conflict. But the world of states is not unified and unfragmented. It is territorial and sovereign. There is a fundamental *misalignment* between a unified cyberspace and the far more fragmented legal and institutional mechanisms humans have devised to govern themselves. The engineers dreaming of global compatibility succeeded in doing their part of the job. They left it to the rest of us to figure out how to devise an institutional response.

Nowhere is the mismatch between global cyberspace and the territorial state more evident than in the domain of cybersecurity. As digital technology penetrates more and more of society, cybersecurity becomes relevant to national security, with all that implies for military power and international relations. For many state actors (and many critical non-state actors), the Snowden revelations merely confirmed what they had suspected all along: the United States has hegemony over the Internet, and all the talk about a globalized free flow of information is nothing but ideological cover for its hegemony. When the US International Strategy for Cyberspace says "The United States supports an Internet with end-to-end interoperability, which allows people worldwide to connect to knowledge, ideas, and one another through technology that meets their needs" they see not an ideal, but a self-serving rationalization for a US information empire. Whether those accusations are true or not, it is undeniable that cyberspace is increasingly seen as a place where nation-states compete for power (Segal, 2016).

"Fragmentation of the Internet" as a move in policy discourse

Thus while the Snowden revelations produced the NETMundial's reassertions of the universality principle, they also produced strong forces pushing in the opposite direction. The solution to NSA spying, some asserted, was to restrict the global flow of information. Require companies to store their users' data in local jurisdictions; require Internet routing to stay within the borders of the country; require governments or users to rely on local companies rather than foreign companies for services like email and cloud computing. The call for protection was often couched in the language of sovereignty. There are now explicit demands for data sovereignty, technological sovereignty, or various other labels for some kind of governmental or jurisdictional overlay on information networks. They come from Brazil, Germany, the UK, and the European Commission as well as from China, Russia, Saudi Arabia, and Iran. The message is the same: realign states and cyberspace.

It was in this context that "fragmentation" and "Balkanization" became one of the prevailing themes in Internet policy. The New America Foundation's Sasha Meinrath, a frequent recipient of US State Department funding, complained that "the motivations of those nations questioning America's *de facto* control over the global Internet may vary, but their responses are all pointing in the same troubling direction: toward a Balkanized Internet." A paper funded and published by the World Economic Forum announced, "A growing number of thought leaders in government, the private sector, the Internet technical community, civil society and academia have expressed concerns over the past two years that the Internet is in some danger of splintering or breaking up into loosely coupled islands of connectivity" (Drake, Cerf, and Kleinwachter, 2016). But this problem goes much further back than June 2013. The Snowden revelations merely amplified and exacerbated longstanding tensions between Internet communications and national sovereignty, tensions that had been growing for the preceding 20 years (Mueller, 2010).

Interrogating fragmentation

Once we understand the critical role the idea of fragmentation or Balkanization is playing in global Internet governance debates, the more important it becomes to interrogate the concept. What do we really mean by Internet fragmentation, anyway?

Pursuing that question brings us face to face with a central paradox of the Internet. The Internet is a network of networks; a vast collection of independently managed but interoperable information systems. As such, the Internet protocols (coupled with increasingly powerful information processing capabilities) foster *both* universal interoperability *and* the ability to modulate and restrict the extent to which any given network opens itself up to traffic from other networks. (This paradox is explored in more detail in Chapter 2.) When Vint Cerf opposes fragmentation on the grounds that "universal connectivity among the willing" was a founding principle of the Internet, he glosses over the question: what happens when people are *not willing*? The same paper that speaks confidently of the Internet's "invariants" also notes in passing that the "invariant" principle of end to end connectivity became practically extinct fifteen years ago with the rise of firewalls and network address translators (Daigle, 2015).

Once one starts to wrap one's mind around the technical mechanisms that can monitor, limit, intermediate, condition, or block Internet traffic, one realizes that such technologies are widely used and embedded in the Internet's infrastructure. There is technology to monitor and block packets, domains, Internet Protocol (IP) addresses, or URLs, for both good reasons and bad reasons. Interoperability can be fractured by untrusted or expired digital certificates. Connectivity can be blocked by geocoding of copyrighted content as well as by authoritarian censors. Traffic can be fragmented by a government-ordered "kill switch" or by a routing anomaly accidentally promulgated by Internet service providers (ISPs). Any intelligent treatment of this subject needs to go beyond a religious commitment to universal compatibility and carefully assess the political and economic implications of decisions to limit connectivity.

That line of inquiry enables one to question, and even reverse, key aspects of the fragmentation narrative. Even as we worry about barriers and fragmentation, we also seem to be deeply worried about the prospect of being unable to prevent indiscriminate, universal access to our computers, our data, and our networks. We don't always like being exposed to anyone in the world. The idea of a universal, unfragmented space is at once grandly alluring and utterly terrifying. Those who attempt to air-gap networks or protect things from global connectivity soon discover that this is extremely difficult to do. It is a difficulty experienced not just by households or sovereign states attempting to filter content, but also by military networks and nuclear facilities striving for confidential, secure communications, and by major corporations trying to maintain databases of sensitive private information. In the age of near-field communications and the Internet of things, one could make a case that connectivity is not fragmenting, but spreading virally. Even people who want to fragment the Internet have a limited capability to do so.

Overview of key theses

This book explores the theme of Internet fragmentation. Although it concentrates on the political, public policy, and international relations aspects of that problem, it also looks carefully into its technical and economic manifestations, and uses that analysis to propose some policy directions.

The book makes four main points. The first is that communications globalization is, on net, an overwhelmingly good thing for humanity. It enhances the scope, scale, and division of labor in the information economy; it facilitates innovation; it broadens access to services. That being said, it is also true that various forms of insulation from or filtering of global access can be beneficial. Its benefits, however, accrue only if it is subject to the discipline of end user choice, which creates a congruence between the costs and benefits of the filtering and the entity doing the filtering.

The second point is that the threats of technical fragmentation are overblown. The Internet is not breaking apart. The network effects and economic benefits generated by widespread connectivity – the sinews that hold the Internet together – are powerful and growing. Once this point is understood, it becomes easier to see how in many ways the discourse around fragmentation is a confused or even dishonest one. And this is the third point: the rhetoric of fragmentation can be used to camouflage the more important issue, which is the question of alignment, the perceived need to re-align control of communications with the jurisdictional boundaries of national states. The book opens the door to a more direct and far-reaching consideration of the problem of network–state alignment.

Finally, the book challenges the equation of free, open, globalized communications with the supremacy of the US government. Given the dominance of US firms and the stated objectives of American policy, it is, I admit, easy and tempting to view things that way. But that viewpoint is based on obsolete, state-centric assumptions. It fails to recognize the degree to which cyberspace is creating its own polity with its own interests, one that is not conjoint with the interests of specific states. Indeed, if all we can see in the struggles over Internet governance is the question of which state comes out more powerful than its rivals, then our mentality has advanced little from seventeenth-century mercantilism.

If national alignment is the problem, what is the solution? The book concludes by proposing an unusual way out of these dilemmas: a move away from national sovereignty and towards popular sovereignty in cyberspace. This implies new governance institutions. How do we get there? Nationalism is a way of linking group identities to the formation of political institutions, and is historically associated with the formation of nation-states. Can there be a cyber-version of nationalism, an Internet nation so to speak, that forges its own political identity and provides the impetus for transnational forms of Internet governance? The last part of the book explores that possibility.

TWO

A Taxonomy of "Fragmentation"

On one side we have advocates of "data sovereignty;" on the other we have the critics of Internet "fragmentation" or "Balkanization." One can bring clarity to this debate by asking a simple question: *what does fragmentation of the Internet mean*? What are the conditions that have to prevail for us to call the Internet "fragmented" or "not fragmented," "Balkanized" or not? The literature on this topic contains very few attempts to grapple with that question, and most of them are weak or muddled conceptually.

Let's start with basic definitions. As a noun, the word "fragment" implies a part that has been disconnected from a greater whole, like a shard of glass detached from a broken bottle. As an adjective, "fragmented" means existing or functioning as though broken into separate parts, disunified, dismembered.

How would one recognize a fragmented Internet when one sees it? Herein lies the central irony of the Balkanization debate. One could use the concept of fragmentation to arrive simultaneously at two diametrically opposed conclusions:

- The internet is now and always has been fragmented
- The Internet is not now and never will be fragmented

The unifragged Internet

The Internet could be characterized as fragmented because it was designed to be a network of networks. The basic units of internetworking are known as Autonomous Systems. Autonomy is a strong word; it implies an ability or freedom to act independently. In a political context, it refers to the ability to govern oneself. In a network context, it means something similar: the ability to set policies for naming, addressing and routing, and to control or manage many other aspects of network operations. In this respect, the Internet is already "Balkanized." It is a federation of Autonomous Systems with an extensive capability for selective, fine-grained "secession" from practically any other part of the federation.

The Internet is unlike the Balkans in one crucial respect, however: all Autonomous Systems speak a common language. That language is a set of data

"The Internet is already 'Balkanized' – its networks are capable of selective, fine-grained 'secession' from practically any other part of the system."

formatting, naming, addressing, and routing standards collectively known as "the Internet protocols," the most basic of which is Internet Protocol (IP). Even so, nothing compels any single Autonomous System (APs) to open itself up completely to all others. All APs can exercise – or try to exercise – control over who they interconnect with, what packets they admit into or out of their systems, what services they want to accept or block, what content can enter and leave. And it is clear that many if not most Autonomous Systems are exercising this capability. They are blocking domains associated with attackers, filtering IP address ranges associated with spammers, using firewalls and security software to detect and block malware. In this sense, every Autonomous System is a "fragment" of the whole Internet, a part distinct from a greater whole. As one scholarly duo put it, the Internet is always "locally configured as well as globally networked" (Lobato and Meese, 2016, p. 14).

At the same time, we could say that the Internet is not now and is unlikely ever to be truly fragmented, if "fragmentation" is understood in the harder sense of "broken into separate parts" with insurmountable barriers to communication between them. As noted before, all Autonomous Systems on the Internet use the same protocol for data communication: IP, which includes a globally consistent address space. IP functions as the lingua franca that connects and makes compatible an enormous number of lower-level physical layer technologies (such as copper, radio, or fiber) and higher-level transport and application standards (such as the Web protocol, word processing applications, or instant messaging apps). This is often visualized as an hourglass, with IP being the single, common protocol that converges a growing and constantly changing array of different technologies above it and below it in the protocol stack.

People use IP because everyone else is using it. The benefits of common usage of it are so great, the utility of having at least the *potential* to exchange information with anyone in the world at any time is so enormous, that it is difficult to imagine any organization refusing to use IP for data networking.

Far from splintering or faltering, Internet connectivity is spreading virally. While every Autonomous System has the ability and the right to manage the nature of their Internet access, openness to the rest of the world's computers is the default value in this environment. If Autonomous Systems want their network to limit or restrict access, they have to do a lot of work to make it happen.

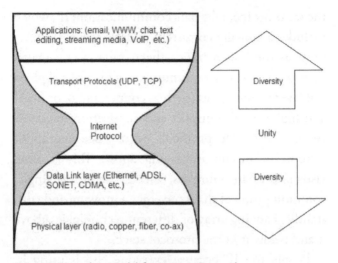

Figure 1: Hourglass Model for Internet Protocol

The Internet is at once unified and fragmented. It is unifragged.

A taxonomy of "fragmentation'

To appreciate the policy implications of this paradoxical mixture of connection and disconnection, access and blockage, fragments and the whole, we need a finer vocabulary. Consider the following scenarios:

- A cable is accidentally cut and suddenly thousands of people are left without Internet access for several hours; is this what we mean by fragmentation?
- A friend provides one with a link to what he calls a hilarious YouTube video. But when you click on it you see only a blank screen with the message, "This video is not available in your country." Is this fragmentation?
- The government of a country orders its ISPs to block domains or URLs associated with content or services deemed subversive or illegal; is this fragmentation?
- A major online newspaper blocks access to its content unless you pay them a monthly subscription fee; is this fragmentation?
- Two major ISPs stop peering with each other and for a day or two, packets from some of their customers don't know how to find their way to their intended destination; is this what we mean by fragmentation?

In some sense, all of these result in something that might be called fragmentation in the sense of interrupted communication paths. But blockages and downtimes are constantly coming into and going out of existence on the Internet (and on any network). Some of these are routine, inevitable, and even beneficial aspects of a distributed system. Others are unintended, accidental, objectionable, and pathological. Clearly, there are crucial qualitative differences among them. Figure 2 provides a diagram that helps to sort them out.

The most basic difference is whether the blocking or disruption is *intentional* or *unintentional*. *Intentional* blocking means that someone has made a conscious decision to limit or manage their exposure to the global Internet. It involves things like spam filters, firewalls, or lists of blocked URLs. *Unintentional* fragmentation arises from breakdowns or technical incompatibilities or physical barriers that make different parts of the Internet literally incapable of interoperating. The cut cable, the temporary loss of connectivity caused by malfunctioning equipment or downtime; the use of protocols or applications that simply don't work together – all are examples of technical incompatibilities that are (usually) unintended.

Unintentional fragmentation means: You can't get there from here. Intentional fragmentation means you *can* get there from here, but someone has decided not to let you.

Insisting on the distinction between intentional and unintentional action focuses attention on four critical questions for Internet governance. If the blocking is intentional, *who* made that decision,

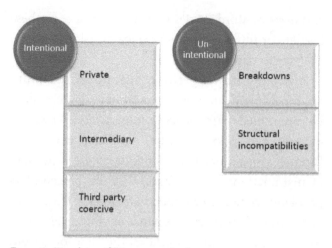

Figure 2: Typology of "Fragmentation"

whose interests does it serve, *who* is affected by it, and *how accountable* is the decision maker to the persons affected?

Figure 2 shows three basic categories of intentional forms of network management that might be construed as fragmentation: (1) *private,* voluntary decisions made by organizations regarding their *own* facilities and services; (2) decisions made by private intermediaries offering service to the public, which affect not only their own property but the capabilities and exposure of their customers; and (3) decisions imposed on private networks, public intermediaries, and users by third parties such as governments; these barriers or filters arise from policy decisions and are coercive in nature.

A key distinction between intentional and unintentional fragmentation has to do with its durability. Unintentional barriers to communication tend to be temporary, and thus a less significant part of the Internet's structure. If the limitations are a product of malfunctions or breakages, they are perceived as problems to be corrected, and are quickly fixed most of the time. If they are a product of what I call structural technical incompatibilities, they last longer but are perceived as bothersome and tend to incentivize the development of technologies and methods capable of bridging the gap. The streaming media players of Apple and Microsoft, for example, used to be completely incompatible, but now there are a number of bridging technologies and each side has made an effort to enable its player to be able to read files produced by the other.

Intentional blockages, on the other hand, can be more persistent. They are there because someone wants them to be there. They, too, will generate technical and social efforts to overcome or circumvent them. But in contrast to the unintentional barriers, efforts to circumvent intentional barriers will result in political, economic, or social *conflict* between those who want to abolish the barrier and those who want to keep it in place.

By invoking the term *fragmentation*, some critics of data sovereignty often make it sound as if their opponents are proposing to eliminate connectivity among networks or cut their countries off from the Internet entirely.[1] This is rarely if ever the case, even when we are talking about so-called "national Internets" (see Chapter 3). Indeed, much of the rhetorical force of the fragmentation/Balkanization charge comes from conflating *intentional* and *unintentional* fragmentation, and by equating *selective* barriers with wholesale disconnection from the Internet.

By confusing these things, or by deliberately blurring the lines between them, the advocates of information globalization may win some cheap, short-term rhetorical battles, but they risk losing the war. Private networks, autonomous systems with the ability to select who and what they access, are the building blocks of the Internet. Private decisions to block very specific kinds of access or content are as much a part of the nature of the Internet as universal compatibility. An indiscriminate attack on any form of deviation from universal connectivity can backfire, by blurring or eliminating the distinction between third-party-imposed, state-level fragmentation and the more granular, accountable, user- and market-driven decisions of network operators and their users.

The distinctions embodied in Figure 2 help to clarify the debate over fragmentation, Balkanization, and sovereignty in cyberspace. It is based on a deeper understanding of the Internet as unifragged, and focuses the debate upon who or what is the unit of governance that makes and enforces the policies that create intentional and selective forms of "fragmentation." The debates most relevant to Internet governance are about, or should be about, access restrictions that are *intentional*, and about *who* is making them *for whom*. Chapters 5 and 6 take up these questions in more detail.

This approach also allows us to dispose of some of the more obvious fallacies of the fragmentation discourse. Some participants in the fragmentation debate have claimed that "the digital divide" is an example of fragmentation (Internet Society, 2016). While it is certainly true that those who have no access to the Internet are not able to communicate over the Internet, it is absurd to bundle this problem – which is both undesired and unintended – with intentional decisions to block users from accessing services or content that they are fully equipped to reach. Access limitations caused by a lack of development constitute a *limited* Internet, but not a fragmented one. Besides, if less than universal penetration constitutes fragmentation, then we should all be cheering about progress rather than bemoaning a fragmentation "problem," because in the past dozen years the percentage of the world's population with Internet access has tripled, and now stands near 50%.

Another writer has claimed that the Internet is fragmented because its users speak and read different languages and scripts (Hill, 2012). The human mind is redefined as a "layer" in the protocol stack, and the psychological and cultural factors that produce linguistic incompatibilities are framed as an Internet governance issue. This is just sheer conceptual confusion. But even if one takes this idea seriously, the trend lines point toward greater compatibility, and less fragmentation. Increasingly powerful information technology is bridging language barriers via Internet applications such as Google translate.

Alignment vs. globalization

Since the Internet has been unifragged from the beginning, and there is scant evidence that it is more fragmented now than it was ten years ago, it should be clear that the current popularity of terms like "fragmentation," "data sovereignty," and "Balkanization" are primarily rhetorical moves. The real debate is not about fragmentation *per se* (although it very much is about sovereignty). It is a power struggle about which units of the Internet are truly autonomous (self-governing) and which ones are subordinate. To be more precise, it is a debate between those who favor greater *alignment* between territorial states and the administrative units of the Internet on the one hand, and those who favor a regime that devolves more authority to voluntary transactions among the users and suppliers of Internet services on the other. As one scholarly paper put it, the so-called fragmentation debate is about "the subjugation of the cyber domain to local jurisdictions" (Polatin-Reuben and Wright, 2014).

The advocates of *alignment* or *subjugation* want to collapse the Internet's open-ended and expanding structure of 50,000+ Autonomous Systems into a structure that conforms to the numerically smaller, more controlled and concentrated system of sovereign states. They want the basic governing unit of the Internet to be the decisions of the state.

The advocates of information *self-determination*, on the other hand, look beyond the state to the

Internet community itself for the key decisions. They want online services and the flow of information to fully exploit the freedom of access, the economies of scale and scope, the capabilities for specialization and division of labor, and the potential for innovation (both economic and sociocultural) that information technology enables. They want the Internet to be governed more by technical efficiency and user demand than by conformity to jurisdictional requirements. For this to happen, governance of information flows must be detached from those legacy political units and devolved to the communicating parties themselves.

Redefining the controversy in this way – as a choice between alignment and self-determination – is highly consequential. It clarifies what the real policy and economic issues are, and it reveals who is really on which side of this controversy. To choose some deliberately provocative examples, hard-core European data protection advocates who want to border information flows, many cyber-warriors in the US military, and the Chinese Communist Party are all partisans of alignment. Whether they know it or not, whether they accept it or not, in most respects they are on the same side in the Internet governance battles.

Exemplar of alignment: the Chinese DNS proposal

What are the implications of alignment, and why might it be a bad thing? There is no better example of the technical and political dynamics of "fragmentation" and alignment than an unsuccessful Internet Engineering Task Force (IETF) standard proposed by some Chinese engineers back in 2012. The proposed standard document, known as an RFC, is entitled "DNS Extension for Autonomous Internet (AIP)" (Diao, Diao, and Liao, 2012). The RFC is a straightforward attempt to cram the entire domain name system (DNS) into the mold of the nation-state system. Even though the proposal went nowhere in the IETF, the RFC provides insight into who would gain and who would lose from strengthened alignment between the Internet and the nation-state system.

The DNS is in many respects at the heart of the Internet fragmentation vs. sovereignty debate. The Internet technical community considers the DNS's ability to provide universal naming "a primary source of the Internet's value as a single, unified, global communications network" (Crocker, Dagon, Kaminsky, McPherson, and Vixie, 2011). In order to preserve its globalized nature, the US and the Internet technical community created a global institution, ICANN, to coordinate and make public policy for the DNS. In order to insulate it from jurisdictional differences, ICANN was incorporated as a nongovernmental, private nonprofit (in what later came to be called "the multistakeholder model").

The Chinese "DNS Extension for Autonomous Internet" RFC proposed to blast away this institutional regime with one based on national units. It described a way to give each nation, which the proposal disguises with the term *AIP*, "its own independent domain name hierarchy and root DNS servers." That would allow each state to create their own top level domains without any need to coordinate them with ICANN or any other global entity. In other words, each country would run its own domain name space and decide for itself what top level domain names (TLDs) exist. There would be no truly global TLDs such as .COM or .INFO or .ORG or .MUSIC. The domain name space would be "fragmented" – partitioned is a more accurate word – along national lines. But while seeking alignment, the proposal still tries to achieve global compatibility. In the Chinese proposal, someone would have to assign a unique identifier to each AIP (country) to facilitate international resolution of domain names.

What would this mean for ordinary Internet users? Under this scheme China would be empowered to assign the top level domain .COM in its own national name space to a Chinese registry, and that registry would be able to assign the domain name GOOGLE. COM (or anything else under .COM) to a domestic website. Let's say that the Chinese GOOGLE.COM was Baidu or the Ministry of Propaganda. For website traffic internal to China, all requests for GOOGLE. COM would automatically resolve to these domestically assigned domains. They would not need to go to a global DNS root. If someone in America wanted to access the Chinese GOOGLE.COM and someone in China wanted to access American GOOGLE.COM, both gateways – the American one and the Chinese one – would have to attach their own AIP identifier to the end of the domain name. Say China was assigned the letter A as a global domain name and the US was assigned the letter B. So the Chinese site would be GOOGLE.COM.A and the American site would be GOOGLE.COM.B. *Voila!* Global compatibility in a jurisdictionally aligned, partitioned DNS.

The proposal would make the DNS just like the telephone numbering standard developed by the International Telecommunication Union (ITU), an intergovernmental treaty organization. Just as every country sets its own telephone numbering scheme and adds an unique ITU country code on top of it when communicating with other jurisdictions (such as +1 for the USA and +41 for Switzerland), so under the Chinese DNS proposal every country would assign top level and second level domain names on a national level, and then add a super-root external to the system that would make these national DNS systems internationally compatible.

Note how this seemingly innocuous change in naming structure alters the nature of authority and trade on the Internet. The consequences of AIP for trade and competition in Internet-based information services would be enormous. To establish a global domain name registry service like Verisign's .COM, for example, Verisign would have to go to each individual government in the world and beg for permission to be assigned .COM in their jurisdiction. To establish a global brand for online platforms like Google or Facebook, those companies would have to go to each individual country and apply for the national instance of their name in the national domain name space. Consumers who wanted a seamless, global service, or who wanted simply to choose a social network or search engine based in another country, would no longer have this choice (unless every national government in the world miraculously agreed to give it to them). Startups who wanted to reach a global market quickly would be severely handicapped by the need to expand their market on a country by country basis. The power of states to restrict information trade, to protect or privilege domestic providers, to exclude foreign information sources, would be massively enhanced.

Under the AIP regime, every individual country manages its own domain name space, and power over it would be centered in the national government. This would make it a bit easier for China to configure its gateway to tell people inside its network that google.com.b (the American Google) simply didn't exist. Indeed, it would be possible for the Chinese root to tell Chinese users that the entire .B (American) DNS didn't exist, if it wanted to. As the proposal puts it, "In order to realize the transition from Internet to Autonomous Internet, each partition of current Internet should . . . gradually reduce its dependence on the foreign domain names, such as COM, NET et al."

Note that this proposal does not propose to "fragment" the DNS in the sense that it would make each country an island. A nationally partitioned DNS that is completely cut off from or technically incompatible with the DNS used by the rest of the world was not thinkable, not even by Communist Party technical apparatchiks. A completely separate DNS would be the equivalent of shutting the country off from all international air, road, or sea traffic. It just isn't going to happen. This is why *alignment* is a much better word than fragmentation when describing the nature of the debate. Alignment is all about the "subjugation of the cyber domain to local jurisdictions." Its objective is to recreate the power structures of national governments in cyberspace; it is an attempt to mitigate the globalization of information fostered by the Internet protocols.

THREE

The Illusion of Technical Fragmentation

When most people hear the word "fragmentation" they think about the Internet breaking up *technically;* that is, losing the global interoperability that was its hallmark and the driver of its growth. This, in fact, is one of the main problems with the Internet fragmentation discourse. It tends to conflate *technical* fragmentation with other kinds of limitations and barriers to access. The term *fragmentation* acquires most of its rhetorical force by constructing an undifferentiated threat to the unity of the Internet out of the myriad obstacles and problems that characterize internetworking, regardless of whether those problems are technical or non-technical, intentional or unintentional, short term or long term.

To bring clarity to this issue, this chapter provides a careful definition of *technical fragmentation*, and then identifies the economic forces that hold the Internet together. Once this is done, it is possible to assess how technical fragmentation might occur and the risks of various scenarios.

Defining technical fragmentation

Let's begin with what technical fragmentation is not. We do not want to call the Net "technically fragmented" because someone, somewhere, accidentally unplugged a server, mistakenly cut a fiber cable, crashed a hard disk, or temporarily misconfigured a router. All of these phenomena are technical and all of them can cut off Internet communications for some people. But localized outages, breaks, and misconfigurations happen all the time. They get fixed. These isolated, temporary, and mostly accidental phenomena are minor, localized deviations from the Internet's desired state. Before we talk of "splinternets" or a "fragmented Internet" the bar has to be set higher than this.

I would define true technical fragmentation in this way: There has to be an *intentional* defection from the global Internet, led by a group of actors capable of taking with them a *substantial segment of the world's population*; this defection must succeed in establishing effective *technical incompatibilities* between their part of the Internet and the other part(s); and these incompatibilities must be both *sustainable* over a significant period of time and able to *obstruct communications among parties that are willing to communicate*. Those

43

criteria describe a condition worthy of the grand and provocative label "a fragmented Internet."

Network benefits

What keeps people on the Internet? Any discussion of the possibility of technical fragmentation must start with a recognition of the powerful benefits that come from convergence on a common, compatible protocol. These benefits are known in economics as the *network externality,* or sometimes simply as *network effects.* If politics and control are centrifugal forces that tend to pull parts of the Internet away from each other, network benefits are the gravitational force that holds them together.

Network benefits exist when the value of a product to its users increases as other users adopt the *same* system or service.[2] Since the mid-1970s, when network effects were first modeled by a Bell Labs economist (Rohlfs, 1974), a huge literature exploring their properties has developed. It is amazing that the numerous papers on Internet fragmentation ignore these theories and findings.

The economic literature shows that network growth has a "chicken and egg" problem: a product

"If politics and control are pulling parts of the Internet away from each other, network benefits are the gravity holding it together."

with network effects is not very valuable until lots of people join it, but people are unlikely to join a network until it has a lot of people on it. Put more simply and concretely, no one joins Facebook if they are the only one on it. Once a certain threshold of other users is attained, however, there will be enough benefit to keep users there – and to start attracting others. The term *critical mass* refers to crossing that threshold level of users (Economides and Himmelberg, 1995). The process of achieving critical mass is path-dependent, as the game-theoretic analysis of Rohlfs and the probabilistic modeling of W. Brian Arthur (1989) have proved. A model of network growth will exhibit multiple equilibria, depending on who joins and in what sequence.

The same economic models demonstrate that network benefits make competition among incompatible or disconnected networks "tippy." If one of the competing standards or networks gains a decisive advantage in scope (i.e., number of users and/or locations covered) the market will tip and, in a process sometimes known as the *bandwagon effect* or *convergence*, users will flock to the larger system in order to reap the benefits of the network externality. (If the competing networks are interconnected and technically compatible, then both networks achieve the same network benefits and there is no need for users to abandon the smaller one for the larger one.) By the same token, after nearly all users have converged on a single network, *inertia* or *lock-in* tends to set in (Farrell and Saloner, 1987). Inertia is created by the participants' general unwillingness to give up the network benefits achieved once everyone else has converged on a common platform. Just as a user's decision to join the network was dependent upon the decision of others to also join, so a user's decision to abandon a network for an incompatible alternative will be strongly affected by the level of network benefits he might have to sacrifice by moving to a new network.

The Internet reached critical mass back in the early 1990s, when it displaced many proprietary data communication protocols and snuffed the life out of OSI, the competing open protocol suite developed by Europe-centered international organizations. Similarly, the World Wide Web built upon the Internet platform to unify standards for content display and distribution, providing a common graphical user interface and document linking protocol across different devices, operating systems, and networks. Today, cloud computing is further tying together different platforms, devices, and operating systems. In general, compatibility and connectedness are *growing* in the world of information technology. The adoption of Internet access is still expanding rapidly in those parts of the world where it is not already saturated. There is still rapid growth in the number of users, in the number of Internet-enabled devices, in the amount of data exchanged, and in the number of applications and services run over the Internet.

Now let's examine the alleged threats of technical fragmentation.

National Internets

From time to time various countries talk of seceding from the global Internet and creating a "national Internet." Two countries in particular, Russia and Iran, are reputed to be doing so. Both are authoritarian states that view the Internet and the United States as conjoined risks to their sovereignty.

What is meant by a national Internet? Wikipedia defines them as "an Internet protocol-based walled garden network maintained by a nation state as a national substitute for the global Internet, with the aim of controlling and monitoring the communications of its inhabitants, as well as restricting their access to outside media." This definition, like almost every other attempt to define the concept of a national Internet, does not clearly distinguish between a technically fragmented Internet and an Internet that, like China's, is technically compatible but heavily filtered. In other words, we must ask whether the so-called "national Internet" is merely restricting access to some outside media, or is literally a "substitute for" or "isolated from" the global Internet? The latter would qualify as technical fragmentation, according to our definition; the former would not. As noted earlier, all networks on the Internet are globally connected but locally configured. The assertion of authority by the state over local configuration constitutes *alignment*, but not necessarily technical *fragmentation*. Only if the national Internet is literally unable to communicate with the rest of the Internet can we call it technical fragmentation.

It is easy also to confuse a "national Internet" with private IP-based networks that are insulated from the global public Internet for security reasons. Private Intranets can and often do exist in countries with full access to the public Internet. The US Defense Department's SIPRNet, the Secret Internet Protocol Router Network for classified information, is an example. Private, closed networks were always contemplated by and facilitated by the Internet protocols. A government department or company that sets up closed networks for secure internal use is not "fragmenting the Internet."

In 2012 there were predictions that national Internets were the wave of the future. One journalist claimed that "... most countries, including the US, will eventually shut down the World Wide Web and instead use the technologies developed by the Internet community to cocoon itself" (Dvorak, 2012). But what has actually happened?

In 2006, Iran's Telecommunications Minister Mohammad Soleimani announced that a "National Information Network" would be launched in two or three years. According to Iran's five-year plan for 2011–2015, "The country's National Information Network should be an IP-based Internet supported by data centers that are completely undetectable and impenetrable by foreign sources. ..." (International Campaign for Human rights in Iran, 2014). After the codification of the development plan, Reza Taghipour, Minister of Information and Communications Technology, and other government officials began a public campaign extoling the virtues of a "Halal" Internet which would be in compliance with Shiite Islamic laws and isolated from the World Wide Web. This definition of the National Network was solidified in the Supreme Cyberspace Council's meeting on December 24, 2013. Research by Anderson (2012) claimed to have discovered a "hidden network" within Iran based on the use of private IP addresses, but was not able to conclude that it was part of a plan to create a sealed-off national Internet. Such arrangements might, for example, be a byproduct of technical arrangements to conserve scarce IPv4 addresses.

Similar noises have emanated from Russia, provoked in part by the Arab Spring and reinforced by the return of Vladimir Putin to office in 2012. Attempts to assert state control over various aspects of the Russian Internet – the .RU top level domain, data localization laws, website blocking, a national operating system – have been accelerating for the past five years (Nocetti, 2015). In April 2014, however, the goal of a so-called national Internet was explicitly voiced by a member of the Duma. Russian Senator Maksim Kavdzharadze called upon Russia to institute its own Internet separate from the United States and Europe (Rothrock, 2014). This idea seemed to have support in the Duma's Information Policy Committee.

If one looks more closely at national Internet initiatives, however, one finds that they are either political rhetoric or efforts by nations to produce and distribute domestic content. They fall far short of technical fragmentation. Russia has not cut off its Internet from the rest of the world; indeed, the Senator's call for autarky, according to one news source, does not seem to have been taken seriously even in Russia (Rothrock, 2014). As for Iran, late in 2016 the government announced the "unveiling" of its national Internet, or Shoma (Alimardani, 2016). But the public documents describing it boast only of creating "an economy for local content" and position it as the vehicle for offering key public services such as healthcare, utilities, and education over the web. Authorities are explicitly stating that the Shoma will not interfere with Iranians' access to the global Internet (ibid.). While it will not fragment, it will strengthen alignment: there is speculation that discriminatory pricing of the bandwidth for domestic versus international Internet connections is intended to encourage Persian websites to move their hosting to Iran, which would make it easier for the Iranian government to shut them down if needed.

One could claim that North Korea does maintain a regime of technical fragmentation. Instead of the global Internet and Web, North Korea has an isolated intranet which only allows users access to a small number of government-sanctioned websites. The few North Koreans who are granted full global Internet access — including some members of the government and military, IT technicians, and computer science students — get it only in public settings under close supervision (Associated Press, 2015). Although there are now more than two million mobile phone users in North Korea, their Internet-enabled phones can only access the domestic intranet and they cannot make international voice calls.

The bordered North Korean intranet achieves both technical fragmentation and *alignment*. But as far as this writer knows, this is the only case that comes close to that pure realization of the Westphalian paradigm – and it is a small, isolated, extremely poor Stalinist dictatorship. But even here, the claim that we are facing a trend toward technical fragmentation is questionable. North Korea is not "withdrawing" from the Internet – it was never on it to begin with. If anything, connectivity within and to the country has expanded dramatically in recent years. Note that even North Korea's intranet is using the global Internet protocols. The growth of mobile phones, the potential penetration of that market by smart phones, and the allowance of Internet access to a small but extensible number of privileged people all indicate that maintaining North Korea's current degree of technical isolation will become harder as time passes.

Kill switches

"Kill switch" is the *nom de jour* for the state's authority to shut down network functions nationally or in particular regions or localities. In September 2014, Russia's Security Council considered a bill that could allow the Kremlin to switch off Russia's Internet in an emergency, such as a war or large-scale protests. In March 2015, the Congolese Interior Minister ordered telecommunications companies to cut all mobile phone, text message, and Internet service for at least 48 hours in order to prevent "illegal" reporting of election results. Venezuela's embattled Maduro regime shut it down in February 2014 as it faced widespread protests. The most famous kill switch case was Egypt's, which shut down its Internet for five days during the Arab Spring uprisings of 2011.

Lest we fall into the comfortable pattern of selectively blaming authoritarian developing-world countries for all the world's Internet governance maladies, it is important to add that major democratic countries such as the USA and UK have also considered shutdowns, and may have executed some. For example, the US actively debated kill switch legislation from 2009 to 2011 until the example of Egypt discredited the concept. In 2011 a panicky UK Conservative government mulled over the idea of suspending social media services in response to the August 2011 riots in the Tottenham area of London.

Shutdowns certainly fragment connectivity. They are also a gross violation of human rights. In 2015, the United Nations Special Rapporteur on Freedom of Opinion and Expression, along with four other international organizations, declared that Internet kill switches can never be justified under international human rights law, even in times of conflict, because any restrictions on online speech must be necessary and proportionate to achieve a legitimate purpose, and shutdowns disproportionately impact all users (Article 19 et al., 2015).

As awful as the concept of kill switches are, however, in most respects they cannot be considered true technical fragmentation. This is because they are a *temporary* condition rather than a durable structural feature of the Internet. Typically they last for a few days or merely a few hours. They represent not so much a desired, stable state but a panic-stricken emergency measure. Further, the more connected a country becomes, the greater the costs imposed on the country initiating it. Egypt's five-day shutdown, for example, is estimated to have cost $90 million in lost revenue to the communication service providers alone, and had strong but difficult to measure secondary impacts on e-commerce, tourism, call centers, and the IT services and outsourcing industries. The Organization for Economic Co-operation and Development (OECD) wrote that "The shutdown may impact negatively on foreign direct investment in the ICT sector and industries that rely on stable communications and the Internet."

Thus while the risk of Internet kill switches is real, particularly when states start linking national security concerns to control over Internet infrastructure, the cost penalties are extremely high, and they represent not a stable structural form of fragmentation but a sporadic and temporary one.

A split DNS root

One of the most commonly cited potential threats to the technical unity of the Internet is a split in the

DNS. The DNS provides a globally coordinated way to provide unique names that can serve as email addresses, website URLs, and the names of network nodes. A recent paper sounding the alarm about fragmentation claims that a DNS split is a major threat:

> . . . the establishment of an alternate root that has significant government backing arguably would be the mother of all fragmentations. (Drake, Cerf, and Kleinwachter, 2016)

Technically, there are two ways a single DNS root leads to global compatibility and network benefits. One is that it provides a coordinated name space, a centralized hierarchy for assigning globally unique names to users. This ensures that there is no conflict or confusion about who is associated with which name. Without a common root at the top of the hierarchy, different people or organizations could appropriate the same name, which could confuse network addressing.

A single root also provides a globally consistent starting point for matching domain names with IP addresses, a technical process known as *resolving* a domain name. Domain names are just human-readable overlays or masks; the real communication that moves packets from one domain to another uses

IP addresses, not domain names. So the names have to be mapped onto the correct IP address. As long as all the world's name servers reference the same data about the contents of the root zone, then the results of resolving any given domain name to its IP address will be consistent globally, and packets will know where to go regardless of who initiates the query, where they are, what hardware they use, or what ISP they use.[3] Multiple root servers using different, uncoordinated root zone file data would have a much more difficult time doing this.

Currently, we have a single, dominant DNS root run by ICANN. One could say that ICANN has a monopoly on the DNS root, but there is no law, either at the national or the international level, that compels anyone in the world to use the ICANN-operated root. Nor is there any law against starting or operating an alternative root. Alternate roots have, in fact, been started, and some still exist. The ICANN root's dominance is not based on legal or political coercion; it is based on the massive network benefits that come from the use of a coordinated root.

If an alternative DNS root was adopted by a significant portion of the world's Internet users and could stay in existence for a long period of time, it would meet all the criteria for technical fragmentation described above. But how likely is this to happen?

Defection from the ICANN root for commercial reasons has already been tried by multiple actors (Mueller, 2002). All have failed. In most cases, commercial actors merely wanted to operate new TLDs and were trying to bypass what was at the time a slow, expensive, and unduly restrictive ICANN policy process. Far from wanting a split root, they wanted an *augmented* root, a root open to adding new names. But they still wanted compatibility with all the existing TLDs such as .COM or .ORG.[4]

Even the attempt to augment, rather than compete with, the established DNS root was defeated by network effects, however. No advocate of an augmented root has ever gotten past the critical mass threshold. Who is going to pay good money to register a domain that doesn't work for 80% or even 50% of the Internet? Who is going to invest in a registry service that supplies such limited domains?

What about defection from the ICANN root for political reasons? It is conceivable that a national government with a large population, or a coalition of them, could establish an alternate DNS root and coerce their national ISPs to point at it. But even in these cases, network effects would trump the desire to split.

No country has more critical mass, is more wary of a US-controlled ICANN, and is more committed to national sovereignty in cyberspace than China. In fact, a decade ago China created an in-country DNS root that allowed it to pre-emptively occupy TLDs that represent "China," "network," and "company" in Chinese characters. Yet China did not create an incompatible root, nor did it try to lure other countries into a global competing root. Instead, it made its new Chinese TLDs fully compatible with the ICANN-managed DNS.[5] Ultimately, what China wanted from this experiment was not a split root *per se*. It simply wanted ICANN to give it the exclusive right to certain Chinese-character domains, which it had pre-emptively occupied. (ICANN eventually did just that.) Indeed, even the nationally partitioned DNS standard proposed in the IETF by Chinese engineers (as noted in Chapter 2) did not propose a split, uncoordinated DNS.

The inertial power created by two decades of convergence on the ICANN root is enormous. In the past, pressures for an alternate root came because ICANN was unwilling to expand the name space.

It delayed including new names in alternate scripts such as Chinese, Cyrillic, and Arabic for many years. But that issue was taken off the table in 2015, when nearly 1,150 TLDs were added to the ICANN root, with 500 more on the way.[6] There are more than 300 million second level domain name registrations (such as *google.com* or *wikipedia.org*) under the ICANN-sanctioned TLDs, and the number is still growing at around 3–4% per year. Domain name resolution is performed by approximately 100,000 different name servers around the world, and all of the users and operators of this large distributed infrastructure are programmed to use the ICANN root to find information about what domain names exist and where to locate them. If someone tries to split the DNS root, and a random Internet user tries to type the alternate domain name into their browser, chances are very high that their resolver will query the ICANN root, and inform the user that the alternative domain does not exist.

A coordinated root zone is a self-enforcing Nash equilibrium, much like agreeing to drive cars on opposite sides of the road. There are massive benefits when actors coordinate, and damaging costs when they fail to cooperate. A split DNS root is not a serious threat to the unity of the Internet.

Incompatible protocols

We saw in Chapter 2 that Internet Protocol is the narrow middle of an hourglass, the convergence point for dozens of physical and data link layer technologies below, and millions of applications above. Is there any possibility that it could be dislodged from this central role by a new protocol? The ultimate form of technical fragmentation would consist of a new set of protocol standards that were different from and not compatible with the existing Internet protocols gaining a foothold and splitting the user population.

American, European, and Asian government research agencies have shown interest in a "new Internet protocol" for some time.[7] Nor is it unreasonable for new networking standards to be explored. The prototype Internet protocols are ancient: drafted in 1975, and finalized as a standard in 1981, they date back to a time when the first personal computers were just coming out; when modems ran at a maximum speed of about nine kilobits per second; when integrated circuits contained only a few thousand logic gates; when there was no WWW, no broadband, no smart phones.

But our continued reliance on these "ancient"

IPv4 protocols only underscores the incredible power of network benefits and lock-in. None of these "new Internet" efforts have progressed beyond the laboratory. The reason is simple: any attempt to migrate to a new, better protocol is confronted with a colossal critical mass problem. So much hardware and firmware has been created and so many applications written for the Internet protocols that it is unclear what one would be able to do with an entirely new standard. A new protocol would have to take root in specialized places and gradually spread through the digital ecosystem in order to establish critical mass. If it was incompatible with the legacy Internet, it would probably take decades for it to achieve the self-sustaining growth that would allow it to fragment and replace the Internet as we know it. And even if another protocol did take hold, there would be hugely powerful incentives to write code or develop technologies to bridge the two. The chances of serious fragmentation arising from this any time soon are vanishingly small.

Except for one thing. We are already trying desperately to upgrade the Internet to a new protocol standard. The new protocol, called Internet Protocol version 6 (IPv6), was written back in 1998 to overcome the impending exhaustion of the Internet Protocol's address space, which is limited to about four billion unique numbers. The number of Internet users worldwide already exceeds that, and more and more devices are being connected. IPv6 has a much larger address space (128 bits, which provides the capacity for 340 trillion trillion trillion unique numbers). But, in a fateful blunder, when it designed the new protocol the IETF did not make it backwards compatible with the old one.

This means that anyone who adopts IPv6 unilaterally is unable to communicate with the Internet as a whole. The only way to stay connected is for adopters of IPv6 to run *both* protocols, IPv6 and IPv4. This is known as the "dual stack" migration strategy.[8]

IPv6 is not really an "upgrade" of the Internet. It is actually an entirely new Internet being built and run in parallel alongside the old one. It may be a "better" protocol than the old one, mainly because of its larger address space, but its technical superiority does not and cannot overcome the network effects of IPv4. Twenty years after IPv6 was standardized, only about 6% of the Internet is IPv6-enabled. We will not get rid of IPv4 until at least 95% of the world is running both IPv6 and IPv4; then can we shut off IPv4 without major losses of global network benefits. We are at least ten years away from that date. It could be twenty years.

The problem with the dual stack migration strategy is that it means that both Internets – the IPv4 one and the IPv6 one – must continue growing. And that means that the demand for IPv4 addresses will continue to grow. Since we have run out of unassigned IPv4 addresses to give growing networks, it is unclear where these numbers are going to come from for the next ten years. A growing market for IPv4 number blocks is successfully moving addresses from unneeded or less utilized networks to more critical and valuable uses, but as the scarcity of addresses intensifies, there will have to be kludgy technical adaptations to the constraints on the parallel growth of the old (IPv4) Internet. These adaptations can actually create technical incompatibilities that might prevent certain Internet applications from running properly.

The costs and incompatibilities associated with migration to IPv6 raise doubts about whether the complete transition will ever take place. It is likely that it will, but we can also envision a scenario in which the world equilibrates on a two-tiered Internet, one running IPv6 and a sizable segment continuing to run IPv4 and relying on other networks' willingness to run both protocols to maintain universal connectivity.

Ironically, then, the most serious threat of technical fragmentation on the Internet comes not from Russia or China, not from a state-sponsored alternative protocol, not from a split DNS root, but from the Internet technical community's own *failure to grasp the power of network effects.* By designing a new protocol that was not backwards compatible, it undermined the incentives for migration, generated an enormous critical mass problem, and created the potential for structural incompatibilities at the application layer.

Application layer incompatibilities

"Fragmentation" is sometimes conflated with incompatibilities between different applications that run on the Internet. One cannot use Skype, for example, to chat with someone who only has Telegram or WhatsApp installed. Likewise, the information users place on Facebook cannot easily be transferred to Google Plus or LinkedIn should users decide they want to switch platforms.

To see this as "fragmentation of the Internet," however, is wrong. These services run at the application layer of the Internet, and the Internet is based on global compatibility at the network layer. Applications are not part of the Internet infrastructure *per se*. Indeed, the very universality of Internet connectivity gives developers the freedom to offer any competing, incompatible applications they want. This is a good thing – a vital and unavoidable part of facilitating innovation and consumer choice. Users can decide for themselves how they value various levels of cross-application compatibility, and make choices accordingly. With chat services, for example, it is easy and almost costless to install multiple instant messaging apps on one's phone or computer so that users who have adopted different apps can reach each other. With social media platforms, the ability to span platforms is weaker because of the costs associated with duplicating posts, but the issue here is not really fragmentation but the opposite – the convergence of so many people on the same social media platform, which gives the dominant provider inertia and market power. In both cases, meta-apps are developing, that facilitate exchanges of data across platforms.

If walled gardens at the application layer do not raise technical fragmentation worries, what about walled gardens at the network layer? Could the Internet be fragmented by ISPs who attempt to limit the content, applications, or services available to their customers? The answer is obviously no. There are powerful market and regulatory barriers to such attempts in most places. Not since the days of America Online has there been any serious attempt to run an ISP as a walled garden (except perhaps in countries where the government controls a monopoly ISP). Since then it has become clear that walled garden ISPs cannot compete against ISPs who offer the full Internet. Although some ISPs are vertically integrated into a few areas of content, one sees little tendency for them to drastically limit what is available to their customers. ISPs who try to do so have only generated consumer resistance and network neutrality regulations.

Why connectivity wins

Far from splintering or faltering, Internet connectivity is spreading virally. It is now unthinkable to own a mobile phone, a household printer, an ebook reader, or even a new TV set that is unable to speak TCP/IP. The much-ballyhooed "Internet of things" is proposing to extend this level of connectivity to sensor networks that go all the way down to street lights, product components in supply chains, thermostats in bedrooms and household appliances. One of the largest and most socially impactful industries in the world, automobiles, is in the process of being taken over or converged with networking and information technology firms as we head towards a world of self-driving cars. Even air-gapped networks and devices are confronted by new technologies, such as the use of acoustic signals or electromagnetic leakage, which can defeat attempts to isolate them (Guri, Kedma, Kachlon, and Elovici, 2014; Hanspach and Goetz, 2013).

All efforts to reverse the tidal wave of digital connectivity have failed. Governments are making strenuous efforts to block content and services they don't like, and these efforts do have a huge limiting effect on users under their control, but they are still using the Internet protocols and for that reason are challenged by circumvention techniques that get around the barriers. Even new, technically superior technical standards developed and actively promoted by the Internet technical community (such as IPv6) cannot displace the old Internet protocols. While there are isolated and sporadic attempts to shut down Internet connectivity in less-developed states, no nation or group of nations has taken real steps to secede from the Internet or to fragment the domain name system. The issue, as this book has stated repeatedly, is not fragmentation of connectivity, but its alignment with the institutions and boundaries of the nation-state.

FOUR

Alignment: Cyberspace Meets Sovereignty

The problem of alignment is the core Internet governance question of our time. It is the arena for a world-historic struggle between established institutions of communications governance and the new societal capacity created by globally networked digital devices. This struggle will continue for another two decades, at least. Its significance cannot be apprehended, however, if it is confused with pulling the plug on the physical and network-layer linkages between organizations, countries, or continents. While alignment can fragment access to content and restrict the free exchange of information and communication services, it is not the same thing as creating disconnected islands or technical incompatibilities. The risks of technical fragmentation or acts of total abandonment of the Internet are minimal. The problems caused by aligning state sovereignty with the mechanisms of Internet governance and policymaking, on the other hand, are real and imminent. Alignment needs to be understood – and resisted – on its own terms.

We are not, however, having a real debate about alignment. There is a reason why it has been misrepresented as a debate about fragmentation. Very few people are willing to openly question, much less challenge, the legitimacy of nation-states' authority over information and communication. Major multinational businesses may complain about its inefficiencies and burdens, but they have little to gain and a lot to lose by questioning whether states should have this authority at all. Civil society groups may be outraged by this or that act of blocking or control, but often call for assertions of jurisdictional authority when it comes to data protection claims, regulating big corporations, or the right to be forgotten. The US government and other state actors who are putative supporters of Internet freedom may sincerely express their policy preference for an open, global space but are not going to tell China, Russia, and Brazil directly that sovereignty no longer matters in communications. Indeed, if one looks at actions, not words, one sees virtually all state actors, including the US, engaged in alignment processes in both the military and civilian sectors.

The biggest reason why the critique of alignment has been attenuated, however, is not only that it is too hot to handle politically; it is also because it is difficult to conceive of an alternative. There is an assumption that we must rely on existing states as the unit of governance because that is what we have *always* done. To question alignment is to question key aspects of the geopolitical order that has been in place since the nineteenth century at least, and fully realized after World War II.[9] That challenge moves us into unfamiliar territory politically, historically, and legally. Later, in Chapter 6, this book ventures into that uncharted territory. But before doing that there is a need to understand in more detail the interactions between cyberspace, state sovereignty, and territoriality.

Methods of alignment

How would one go about subjecting the Internet to sovereign control? This section provides an analytical framework of the methods. Sovereign alignment currently relies on three basic methods, which I call (1) national securitization; (2) territorialization of information flows; and (3) efforts to structure control of critical Internet resources along national lines.

1. National securitization

National securitization involves the recognition of cyberspace as a military domain and the re-framing of cybersecurity as a problem of *national* security. The shift is founded on the fear that societal dependencies on information technologies and networks create vulner-abilities that could pose an existential threat to the state itself. The effect is to incorporate parts of Internet policy and most of cybersecurity policy within a framework of national security. As cybersecurity is re-framed, the security of the nation-state becomes primary, and the security of end users and private network operators who are com-municating globally becomes secondary. Of course, there is overlap between the security of private organizations and users and the security of governments. But they are not the same thing. The national security paradigm emphasizes the autonomy and military power of the state, which is always defined in relation to the power of other states. In this inter-state power calculus there are many cases in which a government's pursuit of greater power or security for itself actually undermines the economic well-being and security of the people and organizations inside it, especially if they are connected to the global economy.

National securitization is manifested in five sub-processes:

The creation of military "Cyber Commands" for the development of operational capabilities to engage in cyber "war," cyber-espionage, or cyber-sabotage against other states. A 2011 estimate concluded that 33 countries had developed cyber-warfare capabilities (Lewis and Timlin, 2011), and since then an additional four countries have announced such capabilities (Frankenstein, Mezzour, Carley, and Carley, 2015).

The nationalization and centralization of threat intelligence reporting and sharing capabilities. Internet security governance, which used to reside primarily in loosely-organized, nongovernmental, and often transnational associations of technical people and network operators, becomes increasingly organized on national lines and led by governmental agencies. This involves greater involvement of the government in surveillance of the cyber environment, the establishment of national Computer Security Incident Response Teams (CSIRTs), and related efforts to nationalize cybersecurity organizations and procedures. Governments are creating new national CSIRTs, either to replace an existing one rooted in the technical community, or a new one where none existed before. Sometimes they are elevating a CSIRT that was confined to the networks of government agencies to the role of a public, national CSIRT (Morgus, Skierka, Hohmann, and Maurer, 2015).

More reliance on national standards and technologies, and imposition of foreign ownership or procurement restrictions on the providers of "sensitive" ICT-related products and services. Market forces and network effects make idiosyncratic standards and technologies unlikely in most cases, but both private sector and public sector procurement decisions are coming under increasing scrutiny, and so are corporate acquisitions. In the US, The Foreign Investment and National Security Act of 2007 granted the President the authority to block proposed mergers, acquisitions, and takeovers that might affect national security. China's Multi-Level Protection Scheme (MLPS) mandates that core IT products used by government and infrastructure companies such as banks and transportation must be provided by Chinese companies.[10] As of mid-2012, India had a draft policy that would impose domestic preferences in the procurement of electronic products "which have security implications."[11] For any country, the demand by national authorities to insert encryption backdoors taints the technology for users and consumers in all other territories. Germany's 2014 Digital Agenda calls for "expansion of Germany's autonomy and authority over information and telecommunication technology" (Segal, 2016, 154).

The establishment or reassertion of legal authority for network shutdowns/kill switches. As part of their emergency powers, governments seek (or re-assert) the authority to shut down networks and services at a nationwide or regional level. This mirrors the historical authority that states have held over state-owned postal, telegraph, and telephone monopolies and radio communication capabilities.

2. *Territorialization of information flows*

In this category we find a range of technical and legal measures designed to align information flows with national territories. There are four distinct sub-processes here: (i) filtering or blocking access to content, applications and services from outside the country; (ii) data localization requirements; (iii) geo-blocking; and (iv) international recognition of restrictions on cross-border information flows.

External content filtering. Content filtering is a relatively well-documented phenomenon.[12] China's "Great Firewall" is the most commonly cited example, but dozens of countries attempt to prevent people within their jurisdiction from accessing websites, documents, or services hosted from outside their direct jurisdiction but deemed illegal or undesirable by the state. Further, numerous states, including western democracies, require global Internet platforms such as Google or Facebook to take down or block content in ways that are supposed to conform to their national law. External filtering relies on a range of techniques, but works most effectively when the country has a few state-controlled international gateways linking it to the rest of the world and the state regulates or deputizes ISPs to implement block lists at these chokepoints. In effect, the state is attempting to define a nation as a single Autonomous System with common routing and network access policies. In many cases, content censorship demands by states make global service providers restructure their services along national lines. YouTube, for example, is available in 70 country-specific versions (and is blocked altogether in China, Iran, Pakistan, and Syria). Twitter uses IP address registration data to partition its feed to display different tweets based on which jurisdiction the user's client is in, in order to avoid censoring globally due to the objections of individual states. In this case, the alignment is transmitted from the government to the service provider.

Data localization laws. Unlike external content filtering, this new generation of controls seeks not to keep information *out* of a territory but to keep it *in* (Chander and Le, 2015). These laws and regulations may require data to be stored and processed only in a country's jurisdiction, and may also prohibit moving data outside the jurisdiction to an outsourced service or cloud provider. Sometimes the data sovereignty concept is broadened to include the facilities and routes used to move data over the Internet.[13] Note that data localization does not actually *fragment* connectivity, in the sense of isolating it from external access; it merely situates the data in places where governments can access it according to the rules of their own jurisdiction.

It is common to associate the push for data sovereignty and data localization to the aftermath of the Snowden revelations. It is true that many localization proposals reflected post-Snowden concerns about US spying. But localization and data sovereignty concerns can be traced back to the enactment of the USA PATRIOT Act in 2001, which authorized the government to request information from American companies regardless of where the information was (OPIC of BC, 2004; Carnabucci, 2011). The term *data sovereignty* predates Snowden: it is associated with the rise of cloud computing in the preceding decade (Vaile, 2013; Irion, 2012).

While advocates of data localization often claim that it is done to uphold local privacy and data security laws, it also has the effect of making surveillance and data intercepts much easier for the local government. Many countries' laws give the state expansive spying powers over domestic operators and citizens. If these governments had to request data about users from Internet intermediaries based in the US or Europe, their request might be denied based on human rights concerns. In addition to enhancing access to data, localization laws can be a response to the costs and delays associated with the use of international mechanisms, such as Mutual Legal Assistance Treaties, to gain access to user data or records stored in foreign countries (Swire and Hemmings, 2015). It can also function as economic protectionism for local cloud providers and related hosting and technology companies. Localization laws can block US or other foreign providers from serving the market using external facilities, and can even require customers to use domestic companies.

Geo-blocking. Geo-blocking restricts access to Internet content based upon the user's geographical location. It usually does this by reading the user's

Internet Protocol (IP) address, and then using IP address registries to map it to a specific location. The address registries' databases show which IP number blocks have been assigned to which organizations and where these organizations are located. There are other, more sophisticated techniques for determining the physical location of hosts on the Internet (Gondree and Peterson, 2013), but IP address-based geolocation is the most common and easy to use. Geo-blocking can be used to restrict access to content, and to restrict the use of credit cards and other payment mechanisms. The most consequential uses are in the online distribution of movies and television shows. Copyright licensing tends to follow jurisdictional boundaries established for the analogue and print media of the past. Geo-blocking allows copyright owners to wall off their movies and music from people in different jurisdictions, which allows them to engage in price discrimination across districts (Mazziotti, 2015). Hulu, an American streaming service offering a selection of TV shows, clips, movies, and other streaming media, is only available in the US. Likewise, the BBC iPlayer, an Internet streaming TV and radio program player, is available only in the UK and is geo-blocked everywhere else to exclude those who did not help to pay BBC license fees.

Attempts to get formal international recognition of "information sovereignty." Drawing on classic ideas of international legal sovereignty, states seeking hard alignment attempt to get other states to recognize a mutual right to make information flows respect national boundaries. For example, the Shanghai Cooperation Organization (SCO) set up by China and Russia drafted a code of conduct that called on states to cooperate to curb "the dissemination of information that incites terrorism, secessionism or extremism or that undermines other countries' political, economic and social stability, as well as their spiritual and cultural environment." This extends the concept of cybersecurity and cyber "warfare" to information content, and encompasses political dissent and advocacy of "subversive" or revolutionary ideas.

3. Alignment of critical Internet resources

Alignment of critical Internet resources refers to efforts to find ways to partition the global domain name and IP addressing system along national lines in ways that provide the nation-state with greater leverage over the governance of the Internet in their territory.

Domain names. As noted in Chapter 3, the emergence of the DNS as a global naming standard with a single global root has generated massive network benefits. While it is difficult if not impossible for individual states to break out of the inertia created by that global compatibility, some states have toyed with the idea of aligning DNS. In Chapter 2 a Chinese proposal to create a nationally structured DNS was discussed. Less radically, governments have striven for years to assert "sovereignty" over the delegation of the two-letter domain names, known as country code top level domains (ccTLDs) that refer to their country. ICANN has not fully recognized states' sovereignty claim, but when there are conflicts over delegations it has shown great deference to the government's wishes. By re-delegating ccTLDs governments can put them in the hands of compliant people or organizations.

IP addresses. Internet Protocol addresses are the globally unique numbers that guide the movement of data packets over the Internet. Any organization that wants to run a network needs a supply of IP numbers that can be used as addresses. Regional Internet Registries (RIRs) are the institutions that distribute IP numbers to users. They also maintain a registry recording which organization has occupied which number blocks, and develop policies for the allocation and assignment of these numbers.

As "organically developed Internet institutions" (Mueller, 2010) the RIRs do not conform to the sovereign, territorial model. They are nongovernmental, nonprofit membership organizations serving multiple national territories. However, in some regions, national governments have formed "National Internet Registries" as subunits within the RIRs. NIRs exist in Brazil, China, India, Japan, Republic of Korea, Taiwan, Indonesia, Mexico, and Vietnam. There are also pressures for greater alignment of the number space coming from law enforcement agencies (LEAs). LEAs investigating crimes often use IP addresses to track down criminals. The agencies want the databases keeping track of which organization has been allocated or assigned number blocks to align allocation records more closely with governmental jurisdictions.

The contradictions of alignment

At first blush, the list of alignment processes and techniques seems very impressive and powerful. But in reality there are many contradictions between political territory and virtual territory, between sovereignty and the global capabilities of digital communications.

Efforts to create alignment do not re-establish the *status quo ante*, but instead create a fascinating set of conflicts. Attempts by territorial states to militarize cyberspace usually evolve into *globalized* surveillance and *transnational* cyber-operations. Attempts to assert local jurisdiction over data or services are transformed willy-nilly into *de facto* assertions of globalized jurisdiction. Alignment also creates jurisdictional shell games: data and facilities are moved to avoid local control, and attempts by states to overcome these shell games can produce intensified forms of multinational cooperation. The effect is to globalize law and procedure rather than to localize it. This is evident if one looks at each of the three areas of alignment in turn.

1. Securitization in cyberspace: global, not national

In 2009, two of the most enthusiastic American advocates of alignment claimed that we are heading toward a "cyber-Westphalia," a reversion to the territorial state in cyberspace:

> With the establishment of borders in cyberspace, everything we know about deterrence, wars, conflict, international norms, and security will make sense again . . . (Demchak and Dombrowski, 2011)

This longing for things to "make sense again" is a major driver of alignment. But have efforts to align states and cyberspace accomplished that?

They haven't. The first obvious result of pursuing national strategic and military interests in cyberspace is that territoriality quickly disappears. Governments learn that the pursuit of power in the cyber domain requires a global presence and global capabilities, and that the Internet enables such a non-territorial approach. As soon as a state is committed to developing offensive cyber-military capabilities, for example, it has committed itself to maintaining an extraterritorial virtual and/or physical presence on others' networks, and to actively monitoring the status and vulnerabilities of foreign facilities on an ongoing basis. Both the Chinese and the Americans engage in global surveillance, espionage, and sabotage operations, for example. Furthermore, most of these networks mix governmental and private users and facilities, so the extraterritorial interventions are not easily confined to the military domain.

General Keith Alexander, the first head of the US Cyber Command, claimed that there is "a common understanding of what it means to conduct warfare within and through cyberspace." The ultimate strategic objective, he said, *"is to ensure US freedom of action in cyberspace and to deny the enemy the same"* (Alexander, 2011). In other words, it is not about defending territorial exclusivity, it is about eliminating barriers within a globalized virtual space. Indeed, freedom of action has a doubled-edged meaning. It could be used to describe something like the freedom of navigation on the high seas or outer space, which implies coordination and cooperation among states to create a sovereignty-free zone. But the term "freedom of action" is also used to describe what happens when a completely successful intruder has broken down the defenses of an enclosed network and can move about it at will, essentially becoming its owner. Ironically, both definitions seem applicable to cyber-military doctrine, and both are profoundly anti-Westphalian.

The reason cyberspace is so radically anti-Westphalian is that in the world of "kinetic" power only the US could afford a military presence capable of projecting its power almost anywhere in the world. Even regional hegemony was restricted to a few. The Internet, however, lowered the entry barriers to global power projection in the cyber domain. It created a public infrastructure that gives almost any well-organized actor the potential for transnational operations in cyberspace. Of course there are still radical differences in the coding, attack, and detection capabilities of different states in cyberspace, but there is no major distinction in the territorial scope of access.

The globalization of ICT equipment, standards, and cloud services is extensive, and would take decades to reverse. Software applications, operating systems, and tools are exchanged globally, so that military-backed exploits and operations can work anywhere and be hatched from anywhere. Governments which try to align security technologies and capabilities with national suppliers are constantly defeated by their inability to reconcile global commerce and communication with national control. In February 2015, for example, Yahoo's Alex Stamos pointedly asked NSA Director Michael Rogers about pressures on Yahoo to build defects into its encryption so that the US government can decrypt it. "We have about 1.3 billion users around the world," Stamos said, "do you believe we should also do it [build backdoors] for the Chinese government, the Saudi Arabian government, the French government?" In a world of territorial sovereigns, any attempt by one government to align basic technological capabilities such as encryption with sovereign power inherently triggers similar requests from 192 other sovereigns, leading to the complete fragmentation of national markets.

If buying Huawei means buying backdoors from the Chinese government, who outside of China is going to buy Huawei? If buying Cisco means buying backdoors from the US government, who outside of the US is going to buy Cisco?

A similar dynamic affects the nationalization of threat reporting. Insofar as efforts to build national CSIRTS are effective, they focus on defending the governments' own private networks. That is, they are built upon the logical and physical boundaries that create borders between one network and another, and not on jurisdiction or geography. But as soon as one thinks of national CSIRTS as governmental authorities supplying the public good of security to all public and private networks in their "territory," the nationalization of incident reporting and response can actually undermine cybersecurity by subjecting information sharing to political constraints and inter-state tensions (Morgus, Skierka et al., 2015). Government agencies such as the NSA are only going to share data with close US military allies, and Russian incident response teams will not likely cooperate with Estonian or Ukrainian ones. The alignment of incident response with states can reduce the incentives of the organizations to share threat intelligence with organizations in other jurisdictions. National security agencies, moreover, may have strong incentives to keep vulnerabilities and threat information secret and exclusive because they think it might be useful in monitoring or attacking their enemies. If security on the Internet is a "public good," the public to which it refers is transnational, whereas the "publics" represented by national entities are territorial and national.

The globalization of the Internet-using public is exemplified by the way NSA mass surveillance practices started to obliterate the distinctions between surveillance of citizens and noncitizens. The intermingling of data from US persons and foreigners in massive automated data collection efforts undermined the fine distinctions, based on identity and location, which had been built into the US Constitution and its surveillance laws (Daskal, 2015). The problem of "incidental" collection of US citizens' data in the course of surveilling foreigners turned out to be huge. The German Parliament's Committee of Inquiry into NSA surveillance in their country (in German, the NSA-Untersuchungsausschuss) found that sharing of surveillance data amongst the intelligence agencies can "launder" the legalities so that territorial legal restrictions on data use can be evaded.[14] Last but not least, the initial attempt by the NSA to justify its mass surveillance by noting that American citizens received critical procedural protections simply did not fly politically. The dialogue about surveillance was transnational, not national, and in that environment few were willing to accept the notion that people who were not US citizens had no rights. Even if they were based in the US, the global social media platforms served millions of people who were not US citizens. Their appeal to customers outside the US would be materially harmed if using their services was equated with exposure to the NSA's spying. In short, the mixing of data and metadata about domestic and foreign users means that privacy protections need to be transnational or they are much less effective.

As for kill switches, one could argue that this is the ultimate sovereign act; total exclusion of external traffic may well be. But resort to a kill switch or Internet shutdown is also an abject admission of the failure to extend sovereignty to cyberspace. It means that national control and the continued functioning of the Internet are completely at odds with each other, and the only way to escape that tension is to eliminate Internet access entirely for a while. Such actions are not a means of exercising power; they are methods of limiting damage, and probably impose heavier costs on the people and the enacting government than they impose on an enemy.

2. Territorialization and the jurisdictional paradox

Moving to the civilian economy, a host of transnational information services have developed around the Internet. Microsoft, for example, manages nearly one million servers in more than one hundred discrete datacenter facilities across forty different countries. These facilities host over two hundred online services. They are used by more than one billion customers and more than twenty million businesses worldwide (Microsoft, 2014).

Cloud computing realizes efficiencies by sharing resources. What matters is not the jurisdiction of the service provider or the facilities, but the ability of the cloud provider to aggregate demand across a wide, heterogeneous group of users. Ideally, cloud facilities should be located where the essential inputs into the service – the costs of hosting, bandwidth, computing power, electricity, and labor expertise – are as reliable and inexpensive as possible. From a few efficient locational points, it makes sense to offer service to anyone, anywhere. Yet jurisdictional alignment cannot help but undermine those efficiencies by requiring providers to put redundant facilities in multiple jurisdictions.

Alignment, in fact, creates a major conundrum, which I call the *jurisdictional paradox*. When governments seek to assert sovereignty over globalized information they have two basic choices. Either they must require every Internet service to keep all of their facilities and data in their jurisdiction and limit the cross-border movement of the data – thereby creating an island that destroys the network effects and efficiencies of the global Internet – or they must strive to extend their control beyond their territory – thereby destroying the whole model of national sovereignty. Currently, we see both sides of this conundrum being played out.

Under the Stored Communications Act of 1986, the US can direct a company to disclose records within its "possession, custody or control," anywhere in the world if that system is operated by a US-based company – even when disclosure would violate the laws of the country where the data was located. The USA Patriot Act of 2001 relaxed and broadened the standards under which the US government could request information. A great deal of the momentum for "data sovereignty" came from other countries reacting to these US assertions of extraterritorial jurisdiction. The proceedings, rulings, and reports of the Office of the Information and Privacy Commissioner (OPIC) in Canada's province of British Columbia from 2004 to 2006 noted that Canadian privacy laws cannot protect data located in Canada from the Patriot Act if it is handled by American firms. It concluded that public sector agencies handling personal information should keep it within Canadian borders.

In its dispute with Microsoft over a customer whose records were stored in Ireland (Microsoft v USA, 2016), the US Justice Department argued that the Stored Communications Act does not "limit the ability of law enforcement agents to obtain account information from domestic service providers who happen to store that information overseas." Microsoft, on the other hand, argued that data stored in Ireland is not subject to US jurisdiction and that it may be contravening Irish law if it hands over the requested data. The case posed a serious dilemma. As legal scholar Jennifer Daskal wrote:

A win for Microsoft would impose a set of territorial-based rules onto un-territorial data. This outcome fails to reflect the unique features of data and would likely fuel data localization movements, which in turn undercut the overall efficiency of the Internet. Conversely, a win for the government would establish a dangerous precedent under which nations can unilaterally – without agreed-upon substantive or procedural standards – compel the

> production of data located anywhere in the world
> simply by asserting jurisdiction over the company
> controlling the data. (Daskal, 2015, p. 397)

The same problem was posed by a proposed change in
Rule 41 of the Federal Rules of Criminal Procedure.
Under Rule 41's current incarnation, federal magistrate judges can only authorize searches and seizures
within their own jurisdiction, with a few exceptions.
Amendments promoted by the US Justice Department
would allow them to issue a warrant to hack into and
seize data stored on a computer anywhere in the world
if the computer's actual location "has been concealed
through technical means." Civil liberties groups complained that the rule change would be a license to "get a
warrant locally, hack globally." A judge complained that
the Justice Department's interpretation would effectively "permit FBI agents to roam the world in search
of a container of contraband, so long as the container
is not opened until the agents haul it off to the issuing
district." In the US, the assertion of territorial authority
means global authority in practice, a major deviation
from traditional notions of sovereignty.

There is a tendency to view this problem narrowly
as an example of the global scope of the US government. But the problem is not confined to the US;

it is a structural feature of the clash between cyberspace and political space. European governments have fallen prey to the same problem in their attempt to enforce the "right to be forgotten" (RTBF). French and European Union data protection agencies have asked Google to de-link all search engine results, in all countries, if they violate RTBF mandates in one or two countries. This would mean that some European governments are demanding global applicability for their local law. They are demanding it even where RTBF-mandated delinking is considered a violation of fundamental constitutional rights such as freedom of expression recognized by other states. Clearly, the attempt to align Internet services with jurisdiction does not lead to a predictable, well-ordered world, a world in which "everything we know about [international relations] makes sense again."

The global technical interdependencies created by the Internet also make territorial blocking and filtering less than neat and simple in its impact. Ukrainian technicians have documented how Russian content filtering, which relies on a blacklist implemented by ISPs, is "exported" to neighboring countries who rely on the same ISPs for transit traffic (NET Assist, 2016). In March 2010, Internet users outside China found that their access to popular websites such as

Facebook, YouTube, and Twitter was impaired. The problem, which was known to affect users in Chile and California, was eventually traced to their use of root servers located in China. If someone lives outside China and, because of network topography, happens to query a root name server hosted in China, that person's queries will pass through the Great Firewall, potentially subjecting the person to the same censorship imposed on Chinese citizens (Zmijewski, 2010).

Geo-blocking does not lead to the same jurisdictional paradox, but it does seem to be subject to growing resistance. The fragmentation of copyright licensing along national lines is an artifact of an earlier time, when markets for audio-visual content were segregated by geography. It reflects the political influence of copyright societies that are organized at the national level. As the production and distribution of digital content responds to the economic and technical realities of the Internet, however, those geographic barriers are breaking down. There are three distinct factors working against geo-blocking.

First, the efficiencies of the Internet as a platform for content distribution create growing pressures to distribute content in a wider and wider geographic scope. The profits gained by segregating national markets are shrinking in relation to the market expansion, greater efficiency, and reduced transaction costs of global access. Netflix's chief content officer Ted Sarandos, for example, said Netflix is increasingly looking for worldwide distribution rights (Spangler, 2015). In January 2016, Netflix expanded its Internet TV network to more than 130 new countries. Its CEO Reed Hastings said ". . . you are witnessing the birth of a new global Internet TV network. . . . With the help of the Internet, we are putting power in consumers' hands to watch whenever, wherever and on whatever device" (May, 2016). The competitive advantages that Netflix gains through globalization are likely to spur other major market actors to follow suit. One commentator remarked, "content creators and publishers are going to need to address the shift to a global model of media consumption . . . for now, we're existing in a liminal state where licence holders want to control distribution, but for little obvious purpose – especially when there is literally no alternative method to consume content in a lot of countries like Australia" (Turner, 2013).

Geo-blocking is also undermined by circumvention technologies. Virtual Private Networks (VPNs), Domain Name proxies, web proxies and anonymous networks like TOR provide savvier Internet users with ways to fool the network's attempt to locate them. Territories blocked out of global media use Bittorrent and other methods to gain access to media content. Lobato and Meese (2016) refer to a "transnational class" who are using circumvention software for pleasure as well as political reasons, and they conclude: "it may be that VPNs, proxies, and other geo-evasion technologies provide a set of popular technical competencies that are, taken together, laying the foundations for a global geo-circumvention system."

There is also political pressure against geo-blocking, especially in Europe. Preventing unjustified geo-blocking is one of the goals of Europe's Digital Single Market strategy. The Commission opened a public consultation on the topic in September 2015. It discovered that 90% of consumer respondents believe that consumers and businesses should be able to purchase and access services everywhere in the EU. More than 80% of the consumer respondents indicated that they have experienced geo-blocking, and the vast majority of them support a legislative solution to tackle unjustified geo-blocking. Although the EU consultation tried to remove copyright-based geo-blocking from the "unjustified" category, the consultation revealed significant consumer resistance to it.

3. Non-sovereign names and numbers

To bring about alignment in the name and number space would require either (1) breaking down the name and number space into national units and granting each country authority over its own part of it, or (2) establishing some new, intergovernmental treaty organization to govern names and numbers. Both options would require the elimination of ICANN. The first option would drastically undermine the existence of seamless global services, forcing all service providers to negotiate access to every other country on a bilateral basis and the complete partition of the naming and numbering, with each country becoming, in effect, a walled garden. The second option would require a strong consensus among states on both the institutional changes and the policies that such a regime would enforce, neither of which are forthcoming. The ITU has been trying to displace or replace ICANN since its inception in 1998, and various states have been calling for an end to ICANN and its replacement by an intergovernmental body ever since the World Summit on the Information Society (WSIS) from 2002 to 2005. ICANN has withstood all these challenges.

In reality, quite apart from whether those two methods of aligning Internet names and numbers with nation-states are desirable, both are simply not feasible any more. A globalized, private sector-based regime for the administration of names and numbers has been in place for nearly twenty years. The costs and disruptions associated with seceding from it are formidable. As discussed in Chapter 3, no major nation other than North Korea is willing to cut itself off from global Internet connectivity – and destroy hundreds of thousands of already-registered domain names or IP addresses – by creating an isolated national Internet with its own naming and addressing scheme. Efforts to promote an intergovernmental approach to critical Internet resources have been rejected, not only by many states but also by most of the Internet's users, access providers, and information service providers. ICANN is well-entrenched, having withstood numerous attacks on its legitimacy and possessing a significant budget derived from its power to levy fees on the highly globalized, multi-billion dollar domain name industry.

In 2016, the US brought an end to the only good argument against ICANN that its opponents ever made, which is that it was not a bottom-up, non-governmental governance regime but a creature of the US government. The special US control over ICANN came from its ability to award the contract for the Internet Assigned Numbers Authority

(IANA) functions.[15] Control of the root of the DNS in particular was essential to ICANN's policy making and economic power. If the US government took that away by awarding the IANA contract to someone else, ICANN would be nothing. The special US government role was always a contradiction and limitation on ICANN's claims to be a non-state actor and a multistakeholder organization, because it gave one government pre-eminent power over everything ICANN did. Yet the US government also provided a much-needed form of oversight over ICANN, making what was largely an unaccountable organization responsive to an established political authority.

Prompted by the legitimacy crisis engendered by the Snowden revelations, the US Commerce Department in March 2014 decided it was time to relinquish what it called its "stewardship role" over ICANN. It proposed to turn ultimate authority over to the "global multistakeholder community." (NTIA, 2014). The idea was to make US policy consistent, finally, with its commitment to the so-called "multistakeholder model." The US proposed to make the transnational community of actors involved in ICANN the final authority over who ran the IANA functions and fully responsible for the accountability of ICANN's policymaking process for domain names. It set in motion a two-year process to give the names, numbers, and the protocol developer community contractual authority over their own respective top-level registries. It set in motion a parallel process to reform ICANN's bylaws in ways that would make it fully accountable to the domain name community, while ending US government oversight.

The IANA transition was a quite radical move. Although ICANN was already an innovative global governance institution, the transition eliminated the last tether to the *ancien regime*. It was a sudden departure from an Internet governance institution rooted in the power of a sovereign government and a move toward a regime of *transnational popular sovereignty*. It was the Internet "people" – the commercial and noncommercial users, the domain name registries and registrars, the network operators who used IP addresses, the standards developers – who would in the future manage and oversee ICANN. Governments were no longer sovereign – they were just another stakeholder in the global multistakeholder community.

Alignment is an illusion

The observation that the Internet relies on a physical infrastructure that is located in a territory – the great "gotcha" used by apologists for state intervention – actually has surprisingly limited relevance to the realities of Internet governance. Territorially placed physical infrastructures do give states leverage, but once they are operational and running the Internet protocols, they are part of a nonterritorial interaction space that often spans multiple sovereign spaces. Speaking of cloud services Irion (2012, p. 48) writes: ". . . how many countries' local laws apply given that the physical establishment of the service provider, the country of origin of the user of the data, and the actual data location could all be used as relevant criteria to establish jurisdiction?" Governmental efforts to bring about alignment of that virtual space with their territorial authority create numerous paradoxes and contradictions: either they must eviscerate the value of the Internet by building walls around their pieces of the Internet (and fight a never-ending, expensive battle to keep those walls from being eroded or circumvented); or they must globalize their jurisdiction, and strive to make their laws and regulations extraterritorial. Alignment is both irresistible for states to attempt, and impossible for states fully to achieve. There is an inherent clash between alignment and the economic efficiencies and capabilities of digital technology.

"Alignment is both irresistible for states to attempt, and impossible for states fully to achieve."

FIVE

Confronting Alignment

The best that can be said for alignment is that it adjusts the capabilities of the Internet to existing rules and authorities. Instead of new and untested rules and messy new transnational combinations of decision makers, it draws on seemingly familiar, well-established institutions and processes. In principle, it allows each country to go its own way, ensuring an overall diversity in policy, and autonomy for various polities. Working against these comforting advantages is the fundamental clash between alignment and the capabilities of digital technology. Alignment undermines the offering of global services, sacrifices technical and economic efficiencies, and limits innovation and new entry into markets. It empowers repressive governments and protectionist interests by insulating people from access to information environments outside their own country. And while doing this it does not avoid conflicts over jurisdiction. Alignment is the digital equivalent of building customs checkpoints, tariffs, and road blocks into the network – with the proviso that in the digital environment the effects of any locality's barriers will be felt *globally* as well as locally. Longer term, it could lead to the erosion of open and uniform technical standards, by encouraging each nation-state to mistrust or restrict access to capabilities that have not been approved, certified, or developed nationally.

Unfortunately there has been little progress in dealing with alignment. One reason is that the problem has not been correctly identified. Alignment is misunderstood as "fragmentation," and policy discussions of "fragmentation" include phenomena as diverse as the digital divide, language differences among people, putting commercial applications behind paywalls, migration from IPv4 to IPv6, data localization laws, and temporary Border Gateway Protocol (BGP) routing configuration errors.[16] With such an incoherent understanding of the problem, it is unlikely that there will be a fruitful discussion of solutions.

In this chapter I briefly examine some of the ideas that have been floated about responses to the so-called fragmentation problem. Due to space limitations, the comparisons cannot be comprehensive, evidence-based evaluations; rather, they are quick critiques that indicate why this book pursues other options.

Enhanced international legal cooperation

One of the most common proposed solutions to the problems of fragmented jurisdiction is to advocate legal harmonization. This refers to reformed, more efficient methods of legal cooperation among states. At its most ambitious this involves international treaties; more modest efforts in this direction include the reform of Mutual Legal Assistance Treaties (MLATs) (Swire and Hemmings, 2015) or attempts to standardize state-based requests to take down content emanating from platform providers in other jurisdictions (De La Chapelle and Fehlinger, 2016).

The fundamental problem with solutions of this type is that they are conservative; that is, they build on existing institutions and try to preserve as much of the Westphalian status quo as possible. They do not ask why we need to preserve that status quo. The previous chapter described the "jurisdictional paradox" created by the attempt to reconcile global cyberspace and territorial sovereignty. Restated, it means that strict adherence to jurisdictional boundaries in the application of states' Internet policies limits the effectiveness of those policies because of the way global Internet connectivity provides ways around them.

The attempt to make the policies more effective leads them inexorably towards assertions of extraterritorial jurisdiction. Thus, the harder states try to assert territorial jurisdiction over the Internet, the more they transgress and undermine it.

Proposals for transnational due process or MLAT reform do not avoid this paradox. They must confront the question of *whose law applies*. Proposals for "transnational due process" tend to ignore the differences in substantive law and legal rights among countries. What happens if a censorious regime in, say, Turkey asks an American social media platform to censor a tweet or take down a website that would be legal in America. If the US applies foreign law to the data/enforcement requests, it is in effect giving these states extraterritorial jurisdiction – not just over the data of the service provider but, more importantly, over their users. On the other hand, if US companies continue to offer the most popular online platforms and the US government applies its own law to foreign requests for data or enforcement actions to those platforms, then it is globalizing US laws and procedures. Many states, especially the authoritarian ones, may not get what they want out of an MLAT request as a result, and thus are likely to continue to rely on data localization, protectionism, and other alignment mechanisms to enhance their control. Even assuming that the MLAT process can be made faster and more efficient, it is hard to see how it would overcome the jurisdictional paradox.

MLAT reform may provide some mild improvements among like-minded western states. But we are unlikely to ever get a comprehensive, binding multilateral treaty around Internet governance as a whole. It is the power imbalances among states and their inability to agree on Internet policy and law, after all, that produces the pressures toward alignment to begin with. Even if all state parties agreed to negotiate in good faith, governments have too many conflicting economic and technological interests, and their political values are too divergent, to arrive at a comprehensive multilateral legal solution.

Jurisdiction-based blocking and filtering of content, for example, is a response to the fact that we do not have global institutional capabilities to control Internet content, and no consensus among states about what should be controlled. A World Economic Forum paper characterizes efforts to legitimate and globalize censorship via international agreements as a form of "fragmentation,"[17] but this is a confusing use of the term. Insofar as national filtering constitutes fragmentation, it already exists in dozens of countries, and is widely viewed as a sovereign right of each country. Thus, legitimizing it via international agreements does not increase the level of fragmentation. Indeed, if governments can agree on what to block and succeed in globalizing censorship, it might actually reduce fragmentation, if fragmentation means different views of the Internet from different jurisdictions. The real policy conflict is about censorship, not fragmentation, and if one wants to respond to and resist such controls, the difference cannot be camouflaged as a debate about fragmentation. Countries that fear free expression and openness to the world are not going to change their approach simply because their critics invoke the F-word.

Another example concerns cyber-attacks and national security. The US and some of its militarily strong allies want to retain the right to respond militarily to severe cyber-attacks, whereas states with weaker militaries want to legally separate cybersecurity from traditional military self-defense and security concerns. The best the international system can do to regulate cyber-attacks is to hold recurring nonbinding talks like the Global Conferences on CyberSpace or the UN Group of Governmental Experts on cyber norms.[18] Bilateral discussions among states may also bear fruit. These inter-state efforts, seasoned with some additional multistakeholder participation, may be able to take some of the rough edges off of inter-state cyber-conflict. But by relying on negotiations among states they do not alter, and may reinforce, the root causes of alignment.

Giving up: Embracing national interest over global Internet

Another approach to the problem opts to give up – to accept and yield to alignment. Driven by national security concerns, this view more or less abandons a vision aimed at optimizing the value of digital commu-nications for humanity as a whole, and shifts the policy conversation towards promoting the *national* interest of whatever state the analyst happens to come from. In essence, these voices see the future as a permanent, low-level cyber conflict among states, in which the great powers compete for influence and supremacy in the new cyber domain just as they have done in land, air, and sea. Alignment, in this view, is inevitable and should be embraced insofar as it serves the national interest.

In the United States, this approach is best exem-plified by Council on Foreign Relations scholar Adam Segal (Segal, 2016). In his book *The Hacked*

World Order, Segal expresses support for an open global Internet, but claims that it is only realistic to expect competing major powers to deviate from that objective. So the US, he says, must respond by adopting measures and policies that strengthen its own cyber-military capabilities. Some journalist reports indicate that this is exactly what the US has been doing for the past ten years (Harris, 2014). Segal calls for policies that push technical innovation forward, but his support for renewed research and development recalls the Eisenhower-era formation of a military–industrial complex. The US, he claims, should "harness commercial technology and turn it into military capabilities much more powerful than anyone else." Note that the goal is not to protect or preserve the global and open character of the Internet, but to make one state – the US – "more powerful" than the others.

But how will superior US cyber-military power induce other states to make their Internet more open and free? The answer is simple: it won't. On the contrary, it would set in motion a global competition over cyber arms, surveillance, and information warfare capabilities, and it would stimulate industrial policy initiatives designed to make domestic technology industries rival those in the US. States who felt threatened by US initiatives would accelerate the territorialization and alignment processes we see now. The closing line of Segal's *Hacked World Order* is revealing: "While the US will continue to strive for an open, secure, and global cyberspace, it must also prepare for the more likely future of a fractured Internet."[19]

The "multistakeholder model"

Others see multistakeholder models as the basis for a solution. To their credit, advocates of multistakeholder governance models recognize (partially) that the problem of governing the Internet induces innovation in political institutions, and they embrace that development. But their understanding of the nature of this institutional change is often dangerously incomplete.

Mainstream advocates of multistakeholder models tend to view it as nothing more than cooperation and dialogue among people from different "stakeholder" groups and geographic regions. Many proposals for multistakeholder governance speak vaguely about bringing people together to solve problems. They usually fail to specify who is represented, what procedures are used to make decisions, and who has

"How will superior US cyber-military power induce other states to make their Internet more open and free? The answer is simple: it won't."

the power to do what in their governance regime. Instead, they simply say "all affected [should] have a voice and method for influencing the process and providing input,"[20] as if involving millions of people in collective action over contentious issues did not pose difficult problems of institutional design. Worse, they tend to view nation-states as "just another stakeholder," an interest group equivalent to businesses, public interest advocacy groups, engineers, and developers. Vague calls for multistakeholder participation generally ignore the issue of how institutional arrangements distribute power among stakeholders. They tend to overlook the fact that states can coercively legislate outside the confines of the multistakeholder institution, and that businesses may be able to forum shop or ignore a multistakeholder venue altogether.

These ameliorative views of multistakeholder models overlook the most critical feature of existing, functioning multistakeholder governance institutions: *non-state actors* are elevated to the same status as governments in the making of public policy. Indeed, they may even limit or exclude governments from certain roles. (ICANN's bylaws, for example, do not allow government officials to be board members.) In this respect, *multistakeholder institutions shift power from states to society*. In their limited policy domain, they are a *substitute* for national governments and thus in some respects they pose a direct challenge to the state's claim to supreme authority over public policy in communication and information. Few mainstream advocates of multistakeholder governance are willing to openly say this.

The battle over alignment, and over the scope and role of multistakeholder institutions, must be understood as contention for power. While states are legitimate stakeholders in Internet governance in their capacity as operators and users of both private and public networks, they also are the incumbent suppliers of governance capabilities. A state-centric approach to global governance cannot easily co-exist with a multistakeholder regime. Fundamentally they are in competition; one or the other must prevail in the domain of Internet governance.

Papers that indiscriminately tout the ability of multistakeholder institutions to solve governance problems typically draw on the successful examples of ICANN, the regional Internet address registries (RIRs) and the IETF. They imply that these organically developed Internet institutions can serve as the template for global Internet governance in other areas besides domain names, IP numbers, and standards.

But attempts to use ICANN or the RIRs as a model for other forms of Internet governance must keep in mind three critical points.

First, ICANN and the RIRs can do effective governance because they have exclusive control of resources that are essential to the functioning of the Internet. As noted in Chapter 3, ICANN has a lock on the root of the domain name space, so domain name registries or registrars must come to it to obtain top level domain name assignments or certification as a registrar. In the case of the RIRs, network operators must obtain globally unique Internet protocol numbers to run their networks. In both cases, the network externality creates powerful incentives for all of the world's network operators to converge on a common IP address and DNS governance platform so as to maintain compatibility with all other operators. In both cases, the multistakeholder institutions impose contractual terms on the recipients in exchange for the resources, and these contractual terms constitute the basis of governance.

No comparable form of centralized leverage exists for all the content, service, and application providers that are available on the Internet. Nor is it clear that we would *want* there to be such a centralized point of control. The whole point of the end-to-end architecture of the Internet is that it enables freedom of action and permissionless innovation for users and suppliers. This implies that there is no centralized point where all the world's application developers, equipment manufacturers, network operators, and IT managers must go to get licenses or approvals *ex ante*; they can simply buy Internet access and go about their business.

A second critical point, often overlooked by those seeking to extend or build upon current MS models, is that ICANN, the IETF, and the RIRs have succeeded in avoiding alignment precisely because the resource domains they govern were largely *sovereignty-free*. The IETF standards that form the basis of the Internet were made without any political oversight and rely on voluntary adoption. The people who develop the standards act as individuals; their participation is not structured to represent jurisdictions or geographic regions. ICANN and the RIRs are private, nonprofit corporations with a transnational "jurisdiction" created through private contract. There is no national or international legal authority over the Internet's name and number spaces *per se*. There is no sovereignty over the initial allocation or assignment of domain names and IP addresses.

The third point is that the scope of governance of

the existing multistakeholder institutions is relatively narrow precisely because it is *global*. These global governance entities serve the high-level mission of the Internet, which is to maintain its global compatibility and interoperability. In some cases they can be leveraged to address some common global problems, such as trademark-domain name conflicts or a few cybersecurity issues. But they do not – and almost certainly should not – be used to micro-govern Internet services, engage in extensive economic regulation, redistribute wealth, or respond to the divergent needs of nonglobal communities for more focused forms of governance. One of the fallacies of multistakeholder ideology is to assume that the global Internet governance institutions will become more responsive and better able to govern the Internet properly by including more and more people from a greater diversity of backgrounds. To multistakeholder evangelists, the answer to every problem is simple: more participation from more people! This is a dangerous mistake. Yes, more representation and participation is needed, but not always at the global level. Cramming more and more participants from increasingly diverse backgrounds and needs into a single, global collective governance entity will only overload the policy agenda of these institutions, and make them more politicized and less effective at handling their relatively narrow core mission.

Multistakeholder models are a feasible way out, then, but only if we view them as competitors to and substitutes for state power; only if they have some basis for contractual power; and only if their scope of governance is inversely correlated to the size of the community they engage.

The main contribution of this work has been to accurately identify the phenomenon that is underlying the "fragmentation/Balkanization" debate. The notion of alignment shows that the problem is deeply rooted in the political structure of the nation-state system, and thus there will be no easy solutions. But at least by clarifying what the problem is, the concept clears the path toward a better discussion of the way forward.

SIX

Popular Sovereignty in Cyberspace

When states seek to align Internet activities with their territorial jurisdiction they are trying to assert or preserve their sovereignty. Thus, the problem of alignment leads directly to the concept of state sovereignty, and the question whether it should (or can) exist in cyberspace at all.

Sovereignty in history

The idea of sovereignty as we know it took shape in the sixteenth century. Jean Bodin, a French jurist and humanist philosopher, is widely credited with articulating the modern idea in his influential treatise *Six livres de la République* (Bodin, 1576). In medieval times the notion of sovereignty or final decision-making authority had been limited to very specific powers, and thus allowed many "sovereigns" to co-exist in the same territory (Grimm, 2015, p. 14). Bodin's formulation, in contrast, afforded the sovereign an overall political supremacy, a *general* power to make new law and to amend and abrogate old laws.

This concept of a supreme ruler, and the eventual settlement on well-defined territorial boundaries to separate the domains of each sovereign, took hold for various reasons. It was a way to restore domestic peace by creating a power that could rise above the warring religious factions and force them into a secular order (Grimm, 2015, p. 20). The new concept of sovereignty supported the establishment of an authority capable of rationalizing the national economy with a common currency, uniform weights and measures, and uniform regulations; it also supported the independence of states from the Holy Roman Empire and the papacy.[21] The notion of state sovereignty, in short, responded to a pressing need to detach religion from the state and to scale up and consolidate economic and political governance.

The concentration of power implied by the emerging sovereign state, however, was recognized as a danger. It triggered two centuries of intellectual debate and political struggle over who or what should hold sovereign power and how it should be held accountable to its subjects. With the classical liberals of the eighteenth century, we see a turn against the implied absolutism of Bodin's sovereignty and the emergence of a concept of *popular sovereignty*. This was the idea that the source of political legitimacy and authority does not come from the top down, but from the bottom up, from the individual human being. Lawmakers were perceived as mere trustees of the people, and the exercise of sovereign power was justified only insofar as it was able to secure the individual's rights to life, liberty, and property. In the famous words of Rousseau, the state was a "form of association that may defend and protect, with the whole force of the community, the person and property of every associate, and by means of which each, joining together with all, may nevertheless obey only himself, and remain as free as before."

Sovereignty and territoriality

Political scientist Robert Jackson wrote "Sovereignty is a foundational idea of politics and law that can only be properly understood as, at one and the same time, both an idea of supreme authority in the state, and an idea of the political and legal independence of geographically separate states" (Jackson, 2007). Independence, supremacy, and territoriality are interrelated: "a world based on state sovereignty is a world of mutually exclusive territorial jurisdictions; a world without overlapping jurisdictions." The implication is that to be supreme, authority must also be bounded geographically. It is the combination of supreme power, legitimacy, and *exclusivity in a given territory* that makes for a sovereign.

That observation is important, because it is the mismatch between Internet territory and political territory which is at the root of the current technological sovereignty debate. Internet communications, and digital technology more broadly, have the potential to be unbounded geographically. The standards and production structures for IT equipment and software are increasingly globalized. Even when they are not global, the boundaries are defined more by network structures and logical/virtual boundaries than by geographic territory.

It is difficult to find a theoretical explanation for the territoriality of the sovereign. If, for example, the state is a natural monopoly and there can be only one provider of legitimate violence, why doesn't the entire world have a single sovereign government? At one level the answer to that question is obvious: human communities are diverse and their interactions are localized, so it is unlikely that all the world's towns, cities, ethnicities, and linguistic groups would ever accept a single supreme ruler. But this fact explains very little about the actual pattern of state territoriality we see in the world. No abstract theory of political science can explain the co-existence of states as geographically large and populous as China and Brazil with states as small as Singapore, Antiqua, and Belgium. No theory of the link between the state and community identity can explain why countries as similar ethnically and culturally as Canada and the United States are separate sovereigns whereas the provinces of India, with major cultural and linguistic differences, are not.

All one can say, really, about the link between territory and sovereignty is this: sovereignty resides in a group of people who form a political community with a shared governance structure that has supreme authority. Its supremacy is normally established and defended militarily. The size, geographic scope, and identity of this community is completely path-dependent and historically contingent.

That historical process is strongly influenced by technological change. Shifts in military technology generate changes in the forms of political institutions.[22] Industrialization contributed mightily to the formation of larger, unified nation-states in Italy and Germany. Some scholars have argued that the militarization of outer space could lead to the "deterritorialization of sovereignty" (Duvall and Havercroft, 2008). We need to think of territoriality and sovereignty not as two sides of the same coin, but as distinct, separable aspects of governance that are contingent upon specific technological capabilities for interaction and control. And we cannot overlook the possibility that the Internet protocols and globalized computer equipment and software standards are game-changers when it comes to sovereignty over information and communications.

The rest of this chapter proposes two strategies for responding to this challenge. First, to arrive at the optimal mix of local and global governance, we need to come to grips with the fact that the nation-state is the wrong unit with which to engage in local governance of most aspects of Internet services and capabilities. Second, we need to search for some appropriate manifestation of popular sovereignty for the transnational public brought together by global internetworking.

Changing units of governance

The Internet combines global compatibility with local configuration and management capabilities. We need global connectivity and access, but we also need local control and customization to moderate its effects. The problem with most prior analyses of this problem is that they assume that the nation-state must be the primary agent for local control. They uncritically assume that territorial governments are the most appropriate units, if not the *only* units, to make decisions about information policy, and that they must make the same decisions for everyone in their territory and embed them directly in the operation of the network itself.

But this is a very crude system of management and control. A far more flexible and adaptive response to the problems of Internet governance can be had by devolving decision making to non-state actors: to the autonomous system, to intermediary platforms, to user choice. As noted before in Chapter 2, each of the Internet's independently administered but interconnected networks (autonomous systems) has the ability to regulate and manage its exposure to the others. Nation-states are too large to make information policy and access decisions for the diverse array of individuals and groups within a society, and too small and conflict-prone to make optimal decisions for the global Internet as a whole. Decisions at the micro-level of control should be devolved to the autonomous system; decisions at the macro-level should be left to globally coordinated standards organizations and global Internet governance institutions rooted in non-state actors. Devolution to the autonomous system and to intermediary platforms would mean that within any state's territory there could be multiple policies reflecting diverse interests and preferences. The system as a whole would be better aligned with the varying preferences of network users and suppliers. Assuming some level of competition, people could migrate from one platform to another in response to the policies, introducing self-correcting forces and enforcing accountability.

Serious questions can be raised about the *legitimacy* as well as the practicality of national governments as sovereign rulers in cyberspace. The value of the Internet is not based primarily on national or territorial interest but on the interests of a wider public that has forged social connections, economic ties, and political alliances in a globalized cyberspace. Many Internet policy decisions affect these transnational connections, yet in national policy deliberations the "foreign" side of those connections are not represented. Established political structures, by their very nature, are bound to represent the interests of national states *qua* states, and national governments tend to reflect the interests of a coalition of powerful domestic actors and interest groups. There is often a large disjunction and very thin lines of accountability between the people affected by blocking and filtering decisions, for example, and the decision maker. Only about 45% of the world's governments are classified as free democracies anyway. Democracies are more accountable to the general public than dictatorships, of course, but within them dominant coalitions of actors prevail and can shut out sizable minorities, potentially even numerical majorities. Challenging their power involves very demanding and costly levels of collective action. Given the incredible diversity of group and individual preferences regarding information, the subtle nuances in differing implementations of network control policies, and the huge number of information sources and applications available on the Internet, there is no reason to impose a uniform set of choices on every national society merely because of the accident of territorial boundaries. Just as we detached religion from the state in the seventeenth century, we need to detach information policy from the state today.

The debate about the legitimacy and appropriateness of state sovereignty over cyberspace is often confused with a debate about the *possibility* of state control. The idea that the Internet was inherently immune from control by existing governments was never valid and was never taken all that seriously by real political economists. The real issue was not whether states had the ability to arrest bodies, seize property, repress expression, or block access to information and communication, but whether they were the *appropriate agents to represent the will of the people who "lived in" cyberspace.*

Net nationalism

The real solution to alignment involves replacing national sovereignty over communications with a transnational popular sovereignty. This would require a concerted change in popular awareness and identification – the construction of a new identity and polity. The political pressure It created would have to be strong enough to remove legitimacy and authority over critical aspects of Internet governance from established governments. It would be, in effect, a "national" liberation movement for a nonterritorial, transnational nation.

Where would the *political impetus* for a wholesale departure from national sovereignty in information and communications come from? States are still very powerful. Some organized political force would be needed to challenge national sovereignty in this domain and stand up for the value of global connectivity and the right of connected people everywhere to self-govern the most critical aspects of their online interactions. It cannot be rooted in or answerable to a national polity, nor can it be a collection of national governments negotiating a multilateral agreement.

These ideas are very abstract, but a concrete illustration may drive home the point. When the US Commerce Department's National Telecommunications and Information Administration (NTIA) announced in March 2014 that it would be ending its unilateral oversight of ICANN, it described its intent in this way:

> . . . to transition key Internet domain name functions to the global multistakeholder community.

Many critics of the transition, both domestic and foreign, expressed skepticism about the agent of the transition implied in that statement. Who, they asked, is this "global multistakeholder community"? The question implied that the community so referenced had to be a specific, formal organization, with defined leaders, rules of operation, and so on – and if it was not, the transition could not possibly be legitimate. Otherwise, how would we know to whom these vital governance

"The most appropriate response to alignment is a 'national' liberation movement for the Internet."

functions were being transferred? Clearly, the global multistakeholder community was not ICANN itself. Although ICANN was asked by NTIA to "convene" the process and provide resources for the community to develop the proposal, it was clear that ICANN was intended to be only the vehicle, the institutional venue, through which this global community would act. ICANN was neither conjoint with nor constitutive of the global community itself; indeed, one of the basic problems this community was asked to solve was to make ICANN the corporation accountable to it. So who was this entity?

In fact, by not specifying a particular organization, by leaving the reference to a "global multistakeholder community" open-ended, the NTIA got it exactly right. Whether they understood it or not, the NTIA was invoking a form of popular sovereignty. It was transferring oversight of the IANA functions to "the people" of the Internet, and providing the institutional mechanisms through which any of those people with the awareness and capacity to participate could construct the new order. The global multistakeholder community was, in the end, any group sufficiently mobilized around Internet governance issues to weigh in.

Of course, there were imbalances and biases in the

composition of this community. There is no need to be naïve or romantic about the construct "the people." It clearly does not mean that every single individual in the world participates as fully and completely as every other individual, and that all of them agree completely with the result. That is impossible. It does not mean that the geographic origins, ethnicities, languages, and religions of the involved population exactly matches their distribution in the world population. That, too is impossible to achieve. It *does* mean that the process was open to anyone and that those who did participate were sufficiently inclusive of the affected stakeholders to make the output an acceptable basis for governing. Whether one is referring to the IANA transition in the twenty-first century, the emergence of national democracies in the eighteenth or nineteenth centuries, or the postcolonial national liberation movements of the twentieth century, in *none* of these cases was a majority of the affected population leading the process or fully engaged in all aspects of it.

The idea of vesting sovereignty in "the people" has always posed formidable practical problems and legitimacy issues. How can a large collectivity, comprising diverse opinions and interests, hold or exercise ultimate sovereign power? If power was delegated to representatives, what would stop those purported agents of the people from usurping authority and becoming sovereign themselves? Some political philosophers, such as Hegel, flatly rejected the idea of popular sovereignty, describing "the people" without a monarch as a "formless mass" (cited in Prokhovnik, 2013).

But this problem was solved, as Dieter Grimm points out, by the concept of the constitutional state. Supreme authority resides in the constitution, to which those who exercise public authority are subordinate:

> In the constitution, the people, as sovereign, established binding legal conditions under which their representatives could exercise the power entrusted to them . . . Exercise of public authority at the behest of the sovereign, which is not itself able to act, is thus the key to understanding this system . . . Sovereignty withdraws into the constituent power and expresses itself only in the act of constitution-making. (Grimm, 2015, pp. 40, 70–1)

One could see the settlement of the global multistakeholder community on a new set of bylaws for ICANN as just such a constitutional exercise. Arguably, one could also see the NETMundial meeting and its principles as a smaller-scale, somewhat less significant and less successful move in the same direction. (It was less significant and successful because it stayed at the level of principle and did not create or enact real governance mechanisms.)

The claim that a constitution reflects or embodies the will of a people has always been real in a very important sense, but also a fiction that must become self-fulfilling.[23] At some point a claim that a state's legitimacy rests on a democratic or republican foundation must be based on a somewhat arbitrary assertion of sovereignty by a self-defined polity, and its validity is tested primarily by whether they "get away with it" or not; i.e., whether the claim succeeds in becoming self-legitimizing and establishing stable institutions that are accepted as satisfactory and used by the people living under them going forward.

This means that the door for an assertion of popular sovereignty in cyberspace is open, if there is the political will and a level of organization required to take advantage of the opportunity caused by the crises and contradictions in the existing system. But three major problems confront it:

- The problem of identity
- The problem of displacing (a small part of) the authority of existing states
- The problem of articulating its areas of responsibility with the territorial jurisdiction of states

Identity

Traditionally, nation-states are associated with forms of group identity that are much stronger than sharing a common communications platform, such as linguistic and ethnic bonds (so-called nationality), and/or a common territory and history.[24] But that is their weakness as well as their strength. The match between nationality and state is never perfect. There are many nations without a state, and many states not based on a nation. Nationalities are often created by states rather than the other way around; states try to homogenize the people under their rule by creating or imposing a common culture, and by reviving traditions and inventing myths of origin (Guibernau, 1996, p. 47). Thus nation-states can lead to exclusion, marginalization and domination as often as they create a cohesive community. Still, there is no denying the linkage between group identities and state formation.

Is the community connected via cyberspace capable of the kind of solidaristic identity sufficient to forge a political unit? Maybe. Guibernau argues that a global identity cannot fulfill two vital conditions of success in providing a group identity: continuity over time and differentiation from others (1996, p. 131). But this is not true of the global Internet community. The organically developed Internet institutions are conscious of their own history and have their own origin myths. Most importantly, they have values and practices regarding the openness of technology, decentralized power, and globalized access to information that differentiate themselves from those who are not sympathetic to or even users of the Internet.

There is certainly evidence of an increasing globalization of contacts. While the Internet-using population grew by 144% from 2005 to 2012, cross-border Internet traffic grew by 1,769%, which means that average cross-border Internet usage per person grew by 665% (Manyika, Bughin, et al., 2014, Exhibit 8, p. 31). A survey across 13 different countries reveals that a strong majority (over 70%) view Internet access as a fundamental right. This view is especially strong in developing countries such as South Africa and India (Dutta, Dutton, and Law, 2011, p. 9).

A transnational community that identifies with the autonomy and freedom of the Internet has grown up in the last 20 years. It is composed of roughly four overlapping parts. (1) A technical community that develops the software, standards, and applications for the digital environment. This includes the IETF, the W3C, and the Internet Society, but also millions of independent developers who congregate in conferences such as DEFCON, Chaos Computer Club, or FIRST. (2) Then there are the cosmopolitan advocacy NGOs focused on digital rights issues and development, such as the Electronic Frontier Foundation, Access Now, and the European Digital Rights Forum. While concentrated in the US and Europe, many new organizations modeled on them are forming in those parts of the developing world that do not actively suppress them, such as India and South Africa. (3) Internet-based businesses, ranging from global over the top service providers like Netflix and Facebook to small, medium, and large ISPs (and their equipment vendors) are another vital and powerful part of the community. Especially when these businesses are global or multinational in scope, they provide a counterweight to alignment and a commitment to global access, open markets, and interoperability. (4) Finally, some state-based actors can be considered part of this community, especially international organizations like the OECD, UNESCO, the Council of Europe, and the Freedom Online Coalition. These state actors tend to accept multistakeholder governance and/or economically and politically liberal policies. One might also consider active and aware individual Internet users part of this transnational community, but that category includes all the other groups, and two of the other groupings, public interest groups and states, often claim to speak for them.

All four of these rough groupings are catalyzed and brought together around governance problems by multistakeholder institutions, such as ICANN, the Regional Internet Registries, the UN Internet Governance Forum (IGF), regional IGFs, and the OECD Ministerials. This complex of institutional interactions forges bonds among the community and reinforces a sense of common purpose and history.

The Internet nation has been mobilized *en masse* during some key policy battles over Internet governance. The most commonly cited example is the mobilization around the Stop Online Piracy Act and Protecting Intellectual Property Act (SOPA/PIPA) in 2012. Though rooted in the acts of a national legislature, the extraterritorial implications of the proposed law were perceived as so threatening that it motivated collective action among Internet users and service providers worldwide. According to one study, "a transnational coalition of Internet users was able to kill two US anti-piracy bills that were backed by some of the most politically connected and economically powerful interests in US politics" (Sell, 2013). Another study found evidence of "a vibrant, diverse, and decentralized networked public sphere that exhibited broad participation, leveraged topical expertise, and successfully reframed a debate and focused public sentiment to shape national public policy" (Benkler, Roberts, Faris et al., 2015). Indeed, the global conflict between copyright protection and Internet connectivity has led to many other manifestations of Internet nationalism, such as Kim Dotcom's attempt to create an "Internet Party" in New Zealand, and the rise of Pirate Parties in Europe.

In short, there is nothing inherently implausible about the concept of a community formed in and around Internet connectivity. And it is only a small step from community to nation. A nationality is just a community that wants its own state. So it is neither impossible nor outlandish to move from Internet community to the idea of an Internet nation.

Some may see the online network of hacktivists, Anonymous, as an exemplar of a nonterritorial popular sovereignty in cyberspace. I do not consider it such an example. In some respects it does embody the spirit: it challenges states, functions as a virtual, nonterritorial collectivity, and has issued a "declaration of independence." But there are two major problems with the group that disqualify it from being a model for, or leader of, a movement for a net-based nation. First, to succeed in displacing national sovereignty, an online movement must pioneer alternative forms of organization that are transnational, stable, open and transparent, accountable, inclusive, and accepted as legitimate by the population. As an organizational form, Anonymous completely fails this test. Its organization is precarious, secret, informal, and exclusive. Its lack of a defined organizational structure or process, its embrace of the nostrum "If you believe in Anonymous, and call yourself Anonymous, you are Anonymous," means that it has no accountability and its brand can be associated with acts that seem more like vigilantism or even terrorism than self-governance.[25]

Second, Anonymous's political objectives are not focused on Internet governance per se. It seems to have slipped into the fallacy that a virtual nation can completely take over and displace territorial nations. Like a traditional territorial sovereign, it arrogates to itself the right to declare war (which it has done several times, including formidable targets such as the US Government and ISIS) and the right to engage in acts of force (usually, DDoS attacks or break-ins). Most of these actions are unrelated to Internet governance issues; they are instead motivated by a grab-bag of causes ranging from supporting the Occupy movement to opposing ISIS to attacking the Church of Scientology. While Anonymous has addressed issues such as censorship and copyright maximalism, in general it takes the functionality of the net for granted and merely uses it for operations around issues that seem popular to its constituency and generate publicity for itself. Its actions are not focused upon protecting the interoperability, openness, and freedom of the Internet.

Displacement and articulation

An assertion of popular sovereignty over Internet governance by a transnational community does not mean the complete elimination of states and their replacement by virtual communities; it only means the displacement of specific pieces of territorial states' authority over global communications. This requires a discussion of how such a displacement would take place, how far it would go, and how the new, more autonomous governance regimes would be articulated with the ongoing functions of traditional territorial states.

We will still need states to prosecute and punish criminals. They will still need to levy taxes on their physical residents and use them to support local police, courts, schools, transport infrastructures, and so on. The object of a net nationalism is to establish new, independent forms of governance for the global Internet, not to eliminate territorial states.

A thorough and detailed exploration of the problems of displacement and articulation is outside the scope of this book. What follows here is a brief outline of some of the key areas and issues.

With ICANN and the RIRs in charge of the global governance of Internet names and numbers, and its reliance on the IETF for standardization processes, the Internet community has already carved out a firm foundation of autonomy at the core of the Internet infrastructure. The successful conclusion of the IANA transition and the ICANN accountability reforms will complete the de-coupling of names and numbers governance from the nation-state system. The presence of the Governmental Advisory Committee (GAC) within ICANN still represents a potential threat to its autonomy, however. The ability of GAC to issue "public policy advice" – in reality, a parallel, state-based policy development channel that competes with ICANN's multistakeholder policy development process – represents an atavistic remnant of national sovereignty within the DNS governance regime. The ICANN bylaw reforms of 2016, however, required GAC advice to be based on consensus, defined as non-objection by any individual government. Given the severe political differences among states, consensus decision making is likely to limit the potential for intergovernmental mischief in ICANN. Also, the participation of nation-states' representatives in ICANN acculturates governments to a non-sovereign system as much as it represents an intrusion of sovereignty into the system.

Encryption is another critical area of displacement and articulation between the global community and territorial states. Encryption technology can function as an important limitation on the territorial state's power, and helps to shift authority from state to society. The global community should resist attempts by states to ban or restrict the use of encryption, and find ways to defy or circumvent such bans wherever they occur. Politically, this requires an alliance between multinational businesses seeking trust and accountability across a global marketplace, and transnational civil society actors motivated by concerns about privacy and civil liberties. Only a business–civil society alliance can prevent a dangerous alliance between state intelligence and law enforcement agencies and the major private sector Internet intermediaries who control so much data. Anti-capitalist movements within civil society will erode a business–civil society alliance and end up empowering territorial states and reinforcing alignment.

Content regulation will be one of the most difficult areas for displacement. The idea that states can assert jurisdiction over content by blocking and filtering access to websites and applications has become a widespread, deeply entrenched practice. The only feasible action here is to insist in a consistent and principled manner that national governments have no sovereignty over content and to gradually de-legitimize these efforts. One way to attempt to displace it is to emphasize the ability of private intermediaries to moderate content, based on user preferences and reports. Another way is to point out the possibility that states who want to make certain forms of content illegal can do so by prosecuting the people who consume, produce, or distribute the illegal content and by taking it down on a case by case basis instead of building filtering and blocking restrictions into their systems of Internet access. For the most repressive systems of territorial content regulation, there are still circumvention technologies and programs that should be encouraged and advanced. Governments can restrict their activities to those aspects of the Internet that are actually territorial and within their jurisdictions. For example, if a state considers child porn to be illegal they can prosecute individuals in their jurisdiction for possessing, producing, or distributing it. If the lawbreakers are outside their jurisdiction they can use traditional means of inter-state legal cooperation to catch them. What they should not do is try to build their regulations and restrictions into the infrastructure of communications.

Legal strategies, as well as technology, can be used to effectively displace the power of the territorial state over the more globalized aspects of Internet communications. Both business and civil society should actively oppose all extraterritorial assertions of authority over the Internet. Microsoft's successful challenge to the US Justice Department's attempt to assert global authority over its "business records" is a good example of this. By keeping state authority narrowly confined to its territorial boundaries, civil society can preserve the exclusivity of the Internet nation's authority over transnational governance problems. This has the added benefit of confining state action to areas where traditional democratic and legal due process restraints can be applied.

Crypto currencies can displace some state authority over the use of money, but there will still be a need to articulate the two regimes. If crypto-currencies become the dominant medium of exchange, territorial states will still be needed to prosecute people who steal money and commit fraud, even if it is no longer the monopoly supplier of legal tender in its territory. Some of the state's past governance functions related to money may be displaced by the non-governmental actors supplying the crypto currency, but it is unlikely that crypto-currency operators will run jails and police forces.

The idea that the Internet was inherently immune from control by existing governments has been discredited. But note that John Perry Barlow's original Declaration of the Independence of Cyberspace was just that: a *declaration of independence;* the primary implication was that the denizens of cyberspace want their own nation, to control their own destiny.

The superficial reaction is to laugh at that assertion. Internet exceptionalism is a mirage, we are told; Internet service providers are based on physical facilities, the facilities are under a jurisdiction, governments rule those jurisdictions, the people who use them are located in jurisdictions. The same arguments are trotted out repeatedly. But when placed in a larger historical and theoretical context the idea that existing sovereigns have dominion over the facilities and people that make up the Internet's material base carries much less weight than one might think.

Existing sovereigns already had dominion over the American colonies when they declared themselves independent. Numerous empires, principalities, and kingdoms already governed the areas of Europe before they were unified into sovereign nation-states. Every movement for political autonomy has had to displace some pre-existing form of sovereignty. Every shared identity that mobilized groups of people to establish a new political unit had to fight off or supersede prior conceptions of identity. If Internet users actually do form a community, a community with its own interests, incipient identity, norms, and modes of living together, it doesn't matter whether existing sovereigns currently have the power to impose their rules on them. What matters is whether they can be organized to assert, and gain, their independence from those rules, or to force concessions and adjustments upon the old order.

1 A lengthy consultancy study commissioned by ICANN purports to study the economic effects of fragmentation. It never really defines Internet fragmentation, but says in passing that it consists of "removing links between networks." This seems to imply that physical linkages between networks (which networks?) will be completely shut down (Van Klyton, Dyrma, Engeset et al., 2014).

2 In economic theory, this feature of goods is often called a positive consumption externality or the network externality, but a more precise definition characterizes them as demand-side economies of scope that arise from the creation of complementary relationships among the components of a technical system (Economides, 1996; Mueller, 1997).

3 There are ways of interfering with consistent resolution. Domain Name System Security Extensions (DNNSEC) is supposed to stop it. The information about where to find the root name servers that are currently recognized as authoritative (domain names and IP addresses) is pre-set in the software that runs DNS. The root servers tell the user's browser where to find name servers for the second-level names, and tens of thousands of independently operated name servers do the work of mapping second- and third-level names to their IP addresses.

4 For example, none of these actors wanted their alternative root to assign the top level domain .com to a new operator, which would generate global conflicts over the tens of millions of domain names

in the .com space. There is simply nothing to be gained from generating that kind of incompatibility, and a lot to be lost.

5 It did this by appending its existing country code TLD (.CN) onto the domain whenever the traffic went outside the country, a technique pioneered by alternate root operator New.net.

6 There were already 280 top level domains, including country codes (248), the classic generics (.com, .net, .org, .gov, .edu, .mil, .int, .arpa) and a few new additions (.info, .coop, .museum, .xxx, .aero, .cat). In 2009 ICANN invited nations to apply for multilingual domains, eventually adding about 50 more. In 2012 ICANN's new TLD process received applications for 1,930 new generic TLDs, and as of December 2015, it had approved and delegated 853 of these into the root zone file. Another 480 applications are proceeding through the process, 560 were withdrawn, and 37 were not approved.

7 I am referring to PlanetLab (Peterson, Anderson, Culler, and Roscoe, 2002); the US National Science Foundation's GENI initiative; and Europe's FIRE and Future Internet Public-Private Partnership.

8 In their initial interactions with other networks, if a network speaking IPv6 learns that another network is also speaking IPv6, they can use the new protocol. But if it learns that the other network is not yet running IPv6, they will carry on the conversation in IPv4.

9 It is common to assert that the nation-state system has been in place for centuries. While that is true of a few major European powers such as France and the UK, which took their familiar form since the seventeenth century, most of Europe's political units took the form of multinational empires and most of the nonwestern developing world was subject to colonial powers. Not until the US-imposed post-WW2 postcolonial order was in place can one clearly say that the international system was based on a society of sovereign nation-states.

10 New regulations introduced in February 2014 by the Central Leading Group for Cyberspace Affairs require foreign technology companies that supply software to Chinese banks to turn over source code (including encryption), submit to audits, and build "backdoors" into hardware and software.

11 Following the Snowden revelations, IBM's hardware sales to China went from double-digit growth in 2012 to a 40% decline in 2013. US political pressures have basically frozen Chinese equipment manufacturer Huawei out of the American market (Hiltzik, 2014).

12 See the three edited volumes published by the OpenNet Initiative and MIT Press at http://access.opennet.net/. See also Wagner (2013, 2014) and Wolfgarten (2006).

13 In October 2013, Deutsche Telekom (which is one-third state-owned) proposed that data between Germans be routed inside German networks. In India, the National Security Advisor asked the telecommunications regulator to require all telecom and Internet companies "to route local data through the National Internet Exchange of India" to ensure that domestic Internet packets remain mostly in India.

14 For news coverage in English, see Leyden (2015) and Electrospace blog (2014). A direct link to the site of the German Parliament is here: https://www.bundestag.de/bundestag/ausschuesse18/ua/1untersuchungsausschuss

15 The functions performed by the Internet Assigned Numbers Authority (IANA) include maintaining the registry for the top level of the domain name system, which includes maintaining the authoritative root zone file; maintaining the top level registry for Internet Protocol address numbers; and maintaining the protocol parameters registry for the standards developed by the Internet Engineering Task Force.

16 For recent examples of this incoherence, see the discussions of fragmentation at a May 2016 panel sponsored by Microsoft

and the Washington DC Internet Society chapter, https://www. internetsociety.org/events/panel-internet-fragmenting and the plenary panel on fragmentation at the 2016 EuroDIG, http://euro digwiki.org/wiki/PL_4:_Internet_fragmentation_and_digital_ sovereignty:_implications_for_Europe

17 ". . . international policy frameworks that provide international political legitimacy for [censorship] also could be supportive sources of Internet fragmentation" (Drake, Cerf, and Kleinwachter, 2016, p. 39).

18 See the July 22, 2015 report of the UN GGE on Developments in the Field of Information and Telecommunications in the Context of International Security http://www.un.org/ga/search/view_doc. asp?symbol=A/70/174

19 I've focused on Segal because he is one of the more liberal analysts. He pays lip service, at least, to the open global Internet, and has a keen sense of what is being lost as we align nation-state security interests with cyberspace development. For a more militant and unapologetic version of giving in to alignment see Demchak and Dombrowski (2011).

20 This quote is taken from the Report of the so-called Global Commission on Internet Governance, "One Internet." http:// ourinternet.org/report. June 2016.

21 "Bodin elaborated his theory of sovereignty in the context of an expanding commercial economy . . . With large parts of what is now France either independent or subject to pope or emperor, the plethora of local customs and jurisdictions were inconsistent with the uniformity of law or royal command" (Andrew, 2011).

22 I am referring to the work of Philip Bobbitt, Charles Tilly, John Herz, and Hans Morgenthau, among others.

23 This idea was pungently expressed by Lechner (2007): "But as Hobbes realised, sovereign authority must be self-legitimising to be logically complete. The state that claims to be sovereign cannot

await for its authority to be legitimised by God – instead it should be its own God."

24 Note, however, that a common language is a form of communications commonality.

25 No entity that wants to play a constructive role in Internet governance would ever consider crippling the DNS to make a political point. Yet on February 12, 2012, a statement claiming to be from Anonymous was posted on Pastebin threatening an attack on the DNS root servers on March 31, 2012. Operation Global Blackout 2012 was supposedly an attempt to "shut the Internet down" as a protest against "SOPA, Wall Street, our irresponsible leaders and the beloved bankers who are starving the world . . ." The plan was to overload the root server system using a Reflective DNS Amplification DDoS tool. A purported spokesperson for Anonymous denied that Anonymous was supporting Operation Global Blackout. But this disclaimer revealed the failure of its organizational form; apparently, you can believe in Anonymous and call yourself Anonymous, and not be Anonymous. http://pastebin.com/NKbnh8q8

Alexander, K. B. (2011, Summer). Building a New Command in Cyberspace, *Strategic Studies Quarterly*, 5 (1), 3–12. http://www.au.af.mil/au/ssq/2011/summer/alexander.pdf

Alimardani, M. (2016, September 2). Iran Declares "Unveiling" of Its National Intranet. Global Voices. https://globalvoices.org/2016/09/02/iran-declares-unveiling-of-its-national-intranet/

Anderson, C. (2012). The Hidden Internet of Iran: Private Address Allocations on a National Network. arXiv:1209.6398 [cs.NI] http://arxiv.org/abs/1209.6398

Andrew, E. (2011, March). Jean Bodin on Sovereignty, *Republics of Letters*, 2, 2.

Arthur, W. B. (1989). Competing Technologies, Increasing Returns, and Lock-In by Historical Events. *The Economic Journal* 99, 116–131.

Article 19 et al. (2015). Joint Declaration on Freedom of Expression and Responses to Conflict Situations. https://www.article19.org/resources.php/resource/37951/en/joint-declaration-on-freedom-of-expression-and-responses-to-conflict-situation

Associated Press. (2015, July 2). North Korea Cracks Down On Use of Internet. *Huffington Post*. http://www.huffingtonpost.com/2015/07/02/north-korea-internet_n_7713994.html

Benkler, Y., Roberts, H., Faris, R., Solow-Niederman, A., and Etling, B. (2015, May). Social Mobilization and the Networked Public Sphere: Mapping the SOPA-PIPA Debate. *Political Communication* 32 (4), 594–624.

References

Berners-Lee, T. (1995, October 12). Hypertext and our Collective Destiny. Online. https://www.w3.org/Talks/9510_Bush/Talk.html

Bodin, J. (1576). *Six livres de la République*.

Carnabuci, C. (2011, November). The Long Arm of the USA Patriot Act: Tips for Australian Businesses Selecting Data Service Providers. *Freshfields, Bruckhaus Deringer law firm memo*. http://www.powerretail.com.au/wp-content/downloads/macquarie/The-long-arm-of-the-USA-Patriot-Act.pdf

Chander, A. and Le, U. P. (2015). Data Nationalism. *Emory Law Journal* 64, 677–739.

Chehadé, F. (2014, January 24). If We Fragment The Internet, "It Will Not Be The Internet As We Know It." *The Huffington Post*. http://www.huffingtonpost.com/2014/01/24/fadi-chehadedavos_n_4635949.html.

Crocker, S., Dagon, D., Kaminsky, D., McPherson, D., and Vixie, P. (2011, May 30). Security and Other Technical Concerns Raised by the DNS Filtering Requirements in the PROTECT IP Bill. White Paper. http://domainincite.com/docs/PROTECT-IP-Technical-Whitepaper-Final.pdf

Daigle, L. (2013, June 17). Provoking National Boundaries on the Internet? A Chilling Thought. *Internet Society*. http://www.internetsociety.org/blog/2013/06/provoking-national-boundaries-internet-chillingthought

Daigle, L. (2015, March). On the Nature of the Internet. *Global Commission on Internet Governance, Paper Series No. 7*. https://www.cigionline.org/sites/default/files/gcig_paper_no7.pdf

Daskal, J. (2015). The un-territoriality of data. *Yale Law Journal* 125, 326–98.

De La Chapelle, B. and Fehlinger, P. (2016, April). Jurisdiction on the Internet: From Legal Arms Race to Transnational Cooperation. *Global Commission on Internet Governance, Paper series #28*. http://

www.internetjurisdiction.net/jurisdiction-on-the-internet-global-commission-on-internet-governance/

Demchak, C. C. and Dombrowski, P. (2011, Spring). Rise of a cybered Westphalian age. *Air University Maxwell AFB AL Strategic Studies Quarterly*.

Diao, Y., Diao, Y. P., and Liao, M. (2012, June 13). DNS Extension for Autonomous Internet (Internet draft). IETF Network Working Group. http://tools.ietf.org/html/draft-diao-aip-dns-00

Drake, W., Cerf, V., and Kleinwachter, W. (2016, January). Internet Fragmentation: An Overview. *World Economic Forum, Future of the Internet Initiative White Paper*.

Dutta, S., Dutton, W. H., and Law, G. (2011). The New Internet World, A Global Perspective on Freedom of Expression, Privacy, Trust and Security Online. *The Global Information Technology Report 2010–2011*.

Duvall, R. and Havercroft, J. (2008). Taking Sovereignty out of this World: Space weapons and the empire of the future. *Review of International Studies*, 34 (4), 755–75.

Dvorak, J. C. (2012, January 6). Here Comes the National Internet: It's Happening in Iran and the US is only a Few Steps Behind. *PC Magazine*. http://www.pcmag.com/article2/0,2817,2398527,00. asp

Economides, N. (1996). The Economics of Networks. *International Journal of Industrial Organization*, 16 (4), 673–99.

Economides, N. and Himmelberg, C. (1995). Critical Mass and Network Size with Application to the US Fax Market. *Discussion Paper no. EC-95–11, Stern School of Business, N.Y.U.*

Electrospace blog (2014, November 23). German Investigation of the Cooperation between NSA and BND. http://electro spaces.blogspot.de/2014/11/german-investigation-of-cooperation. html

Farrell, J. and Saloner, G. (1987). Competition, Compatibility, and

References

Standards: The Economics of Horses, Penguins and Lemmings. In Gabel, H., ed., *Product Compatibility as a Competitive Strategy*. Amsterdam: North Holland.

Frankenstein, W., Mezzour, G., Carley, K., and Carley, R. L. (2015). Remote Assessment of Countries' Nuclear, Biological, and Cyber Capabilities: Joint Motivation and Latent Capability Approach. *Social Network Analysis and Mining* 5 (5), doi:10.1007/s13278–014–0243–z.

FT Reporters (2014, September 16). Tying up the Internet. *Financial Times*. http://www.ft.com/cms/s/0/2f2f7274–3a5e–11e4–bd08–00144feabdc0.html#axzz3H5Xbzx1H

Gondree, M. and Peterson, Z. N. J. (2013). Geolocating Data in the Cloud. *Proceedings of the ACM Conference on Data and Application Security and Privacy* (CODASPY).

Grimm, D. (2015). *Sovereignty: The Origin and Future of a Political and Legal Concept (English translation)*. New York: Columbia University Press.

Guibernau, M. (1996). *Nationalisms: The Nation-state and Nationalism in the 20th Century*. Cambridge: Polity.

Guri, M., Kedma, G., Kachlon, A., and Elovici, Y. (2014). AirHopper: Bridging the Air-Gap between Isolated Networks and Mobile Phones using Radio Frequencies. arXiv:1411.0237.

Hanspach, M. and Goetz, M. (2013, November). On Covert Acoustical Mesh Networks in Air. *Journal of Communications* 8 (11), 758–67, doi:10.12720/jcm.8.11.758–767.

Harris, S. (2014). *@War: The Rise of the Military-Internet Complex*. New York: Houghton-Mifflin Harcourt.

Hill, J. F. (2012). Internet Fragmentation. *Belfer Center, Harvard University*. http://belfercenter.ksg.harvard.edu/files/internet_fragmentation_jonah_hill.pdf

Hiltzik, M. (2014, December 5). Suspicions keep Chinese Telecom Firm Huawei out of US market, *Los Angeles Times*.

References

International Campaign for Human Rights in Iran (2014, November 10). The National Information Network (National Internet), Blog post. https://www.iranhumanrights.org/2014/11/internet-reportthe-national-information-network-national-internet/

Internet Society. (2016, May). Summary Report: Is the Internet Fragmenting, Part 1. Online: https://internetpolicyforum.com/is-the-internet-fragmenting/

Irion, K. (2012). Government Cloud Computing and National Data Sovereignty. *Policy and Internet* 4 (3–4), 40–71, doi:10.1002/poi3.10.

Jackson, R. (2007). *Sovereignty*. Cambridge: Polity.

Kaspersky, E. (2013, December 17). What Will Happen if Countries Carve Up the Internet? *The Guardian* http://www.theguardian.com/media-network/media-networkblog/2013/dec/17/internet-fragmentation-eugene-kaspersky

Lechner, S. (2007, September 12). Sovereignty and Territoriality: An Essay in Medieval Political Theory. *Paper prepared for the 6 SGIR Pan-European Conference on International Relations, Turin, Italy.*

Lewis, J. and Timlin, K. (2011). Cybersecurity and Cyberwarfare: Preliminary Assessment of National Doctrine and Organization. Washington, DC: Center for Strategic and International Studies. http://unidir.org/files/publications/pdfs/cybersecurity-and-cyber-warfare-preliminary-assessment-of-national-doctrine-and-organization-380.pdf

Leyden, J. (2015, May 13). WikiLeaks, er, leaks the Bundestag Inquiry into NSA naughtiness. *The Register*. http://www.theregister.co.uk/2015/05/13/wikileaks_bundestag_nsa_probe_files/

Lobato, R. and Meese, J., eds. (2016). *Geoblocking and Global Video Culture*. Institute of Network Cultures.

Manyika, J., Bughin, J., Lund, S., Nottebohm, O., Poulter, D., Jauch, S., and Ramaswamy, S. (2014, April). Global flows in a Digital Age: How Trade, Finance, People, and Data Connect the World

References

Economy. *McKinsey Global Institute*. http://www.mckinsey.com/business-functions/strategy-and-corporate-finance/our-insights/global-flows-in-a-digital-age

May, P. (2016, January 6). Netflix will Expand to 190 countries, *San Jose Mercury-News*.

Mazziotti, G. (2015). Is Geo-Blocking a Real Cause for Concern in Europe? Florence, Italy: European University Institute, Report no.: EUI LAW; 2015/43. http://hdl.handle.net/1814/38084

Meinrath, S. (2013, October 14). We Can't Let the Internet become Balkanized. *Future Tense/Slate* http://www.slate.com/articles/technology/future_tense/2013/10/internet_balkanization_may_be_a_side_effect_of_the_snowden_surveillance.html

Microsoft v. United States of America (2016, July 14). United States Court of Appeals 2nd Circuit, Case 14-2985.

Microsoft Corporation (2014, June 4). Microsoft's Objections to the Magistrate's Order Denying Microsoft's Motion . . . Case 1:13–mj-02814–UA Document 15 Filed 06/06/14. https://www.washingtonpost.com/r/2010–2019/WashingtonPost/2014/06/10/National-Security/Graphics/SDNY%20MSFT%20Brief.pdf

Morgus, R., Skierka, I., Hohmann, M., Maurer, T. (2015, November 19). National CSIRTs and Their Role in Computer Security Incident Response. Policy Paper, Global Public Policy Institute. http://www.gppi.net/publications/global-internet-politics/article/national-csirts-and-their-role-in-computer-security-incident-response/

Mueller, M. (2010). *Networks and States: The Global Politics of Internet Governance*. Cambridge, Mass: MIT Press.

Mueller, M. (2002). Competing DNS Roots: Creative Destruction or Just Plain Destruction? *Journal of Network Industries* 3 (3), 313–34.

Mueller, M. (1997). *Universal Service: Competition, Interconnection and Monopoly in the Making of the American Telephone System*. Washington, DC and Cambridge, Mass: AEI/MIT Press.

References

NET Assist. (2016, May). Research of Nationwide Blacklist Censorship Effect on Customers' Internet Access in Nearby Countries. Copenhagen, Denmark: Presentation at RIPE 72. https://ripe72.ripe.net/wp-content/uploads/presentations/76–russian_censorship2.pdf

NETmundial Multistakeholder Statement. (2014, April 24). Sao Paulo Brazil. http://netmundial.br/netmundial-multistakeholder-statement/

Nocetti, J. (2015, January). Contest and Conquest: Russia and global Internet governance. *International Affairs* 91 (1).

NTIA (National Telecommunications and Information Administration) (2014, March 14). *NTIA Announces Intent to Transition Key Internet Domain Name Functions.* Washington, DC: News release, US Department of Commerce. https://www.ntia.doc.gov/press-release/2014/ntia-announces-intent-transition-key-internet-domain-name-functions

OPIC of British Columbia. (2004, October 1). *Privacy and the USA Patriot Act: Implications for British Columbia Public Sector Outsourcing.* Vancouver: Office of the Privacy and Information Commissioner of British Columbia, Canada. https://www.oipc.bc.ca/special-reports/1271

Peterson, L., Anderson, T., Culler, D., and Roscoe, T. (2002, October). PlanetLab: A Blueprint for Introducing Disruptive Technology into the Internet. Princeton, NJ: Proceedings of the First ACM Workshop on Hot Topics in Networks (HotNets-I).

Polatin-Reuben, D. and Wright, J. (2014). An Internet with BRICS Characteristics: Data Sovereignty and the Balkanisation of the Internet. San Diego, CA (August 18): *4th Usenix conference on Free and Open Communications on the Internet (FOCI).* https://www.usenix.org/system/files/conference/foci14/foci14–polatin-reuben.pdf

Prokhovnik, R. (2013). *Sovereignty: History and Theory.* London: Andrews UK Limited.

References

Rohlfs, J. (1974). A Theory of Interdependent demand for a Communications Service. *Bell Journal of Economics* 5 (1), 16–37.

Rothrock, K. (2014, April 30). The Kremlin's Internet Annexation. Global Voices. https://advox.globalvoices.org/2014/04/30/the-kremlins-internet-annexation/

Segal, A. (2016). *The Hacked World Order: How Nations Fight, Trade, Maneuver and Manipulate in the Digital Age*. New York: Public Affairs.

Sell, S. (2013, March). Revenge of the "Nerds": Collective Action against Intellectual Property Maximalism in the Global Information Age. *International Studies Review* 15 (1), 67–85.

Spangler, T. (2015, January 22). Netflix Wants the World: Can It Really Expand to 200 Countries in 2 Years? *Variety*. http://variety.com/2015/digital/news/netflix-wants-the-world-can-it-really-expand-to-200-countries-in-2-years-1201411740/

Swire, P. and Hemmings, J. (2015, November), Stakeholders in Reform of the Global System for Mutual Legal Assistance. Draft ms. Georgia Institute of Technology.

Thierer, A. (2014). *Permissionless Innovation: The Continuous Case for Comprehensive Technological Freedom*. Arlington, Va. Mercatus Center, George Mason University.

Turner, A. (2013, May 28). Understanding Geo-blocking: watch whatever you want, when you want. *PC and Tech Authority (Australia)*. http://www.pcauthority.com.au/Feature/344774,understanding-geo-blocking-watch-whatever-you-want-when-you-want.aspx

Vaile, D. (2013, November). A Structured Bibliography on Data Sovereignty. *Australian Journal of Telecommunications and the Digital Economy* 1 (1) http://telsoc.org/ajtde/2013–11–v1–n1/a15

Van Klyton, A., Dyrma, E., Engeset, J., Kovatsova, A., and Liyanage, L. (2014). A Report on the Global Effects of Internet Fragmentation, in University of Greenwich, *Working Paper Series*. Presented at the London ICANN50 Conference, London, UK.

References

Wagner, B. (2013). Governing Internet Expression: How Public and Private Regulation Shape Expression Governance. *Journal of Information Technology and Politics* 10 (3), 389–403.

Wagner, B. (2014). The Politics of Internet Filtering: The United Kingdom and Germany in a Comparative Perspective. *Politics* 34 (1), 58–71.

Wolfgarten, S. (2006). Investigating large-scale Internet content filtering. Online: http://www.devtarget.org/downloads/dcu-mssf-2005–wolfgarten-filtering.pdf

Zmijewski, E. (2010, March 30). Accidentally Importing Censorship. *Renesys Blog*. http://www.renesys.com/blog/2010/03/fouling-the-global-nest.shtml

Index

Index

Index